HOW DO I EXPLAIN THIS TO MY KIDS?

PARENTING IN THE AGE OF TRUMP

Introduction and Commentary by

DR. AVA SIEGLER

Edited by

SARAH SWONG AND DIANE WACHTELL

THE NEW PRESS

25 YEARS

NEW YORK
LONDON

Published in the United States by The New Press, New York, 2017
Distributed by Perseus Distribution

Pages 169 through 170 constitute an extension of this copyright page

978-1-62097-356-1 (pb)
978-1-62097-357-8 (e-book)
CIP is available

The New Press publishes books that promote and enrich public discussion and
understanding of the issues vital to our democracy and to a more equitable world. These
books are made possible by 1the enthusiasm of our readers; the support of a committed
group of donors, large and small; the collaboration of our many partners in the independent
media and the not-for-profit sector; booksellers, who often hand-sell New Press books;
librarians; and above all by our authors.

www.thenewpress.com

Book design and composition by Bookbright Media
This book was set in Janson Text and Gill Sans

Printed in the United States of America

10 9 8 7 6 5 4 3 2 1

Contents

"You tell your kids: Don't be a bully . . . don't be a bigot . . . do your homework and be prepared. And then you have this outcome. . . . You have people putting children to bed tonight, and they're afraid of breakfast. They're afraid of 'How do I explain this to my children?'"

—Van Jones, 1:22 a.m., November 9, 2016

Introduction

Dr. Ava Siegler

THE ASCENDANCE TO THE PRESIDENCY OF DONALD TRUMP, A MAN who seems determined to dismantle many of the progressive achievements of the last fifty years, has shocked, saddened, and frightened a majority of Americans. Some of President Trump's uninformed, volatile, and perilous decisions are likely to have catastrophic effects upon our families, our towns, our republic, and our world. Some of his cabinet appointments have already appeared ignorant at best, and dangerous at worst. And his interactions with both friends and foes around the globe seem destined to heighten rather than abate conflict. Beyond these threats to our democratic way of life, Donald Trump's performance during his campaign and presidency has seemingly validated a long list of behaviors we strive to get our children to recognize and reject, from rudeness, prejudice, and bullying to dishonesty, greed, and shamelessness.

Trump's anti-immigrant, misogynistic, racist, anti-intellectual, anti-LGBTQ, and anti-disabled policies are threatening to all Americans, including children; they are destructive to our core values. His personality is destructive, too. He's impulsive, manipulative, vitriolic, self-aggrandizing, and aggressive, and has a poor capacity to regulate any of these traits; he lacks morality, self-reflection, and self-restraint. And he is not alone. He has assembled a group of men (and a very few women) around him who appear to share his views. In addition, some Americans outside of government feel liberated by Trump's excesses. They embrace his lowering of the national discourse and have interpreted his pronouncements on immigrants and other minority groups as an open invitation to vitriol and violence.

Many members of the Republican party, while expressing private dismay at his more outrageous behavior, seem intimidated and completely unable to speak out against him (despite the fact that many of them were mocked and humiliated by him during his campaign). Those who bow to Trump's threats do not seem to understand the axiom that you cannot accommodate to a bully, nor normalize his aggression. But in a more heartening response, we have seen millions of Americans rise up in protest and resistance.

In the Age of Trump, our task as parents of the next generation becomes more crucial—and more complicated—than ever. We must shield our children from the effects of Trump's policies as best we can and protect them from the worst aspects of his character. But we must also try to explain to them how someone like this could have been elected to the highest office in the land, and why our country seems to have rewarded behavior that most of us condemn. At the same time, we must educate our children to be informed, committed, respectful, and engaged citizens, and we must include them in our resistance against Trump's regime so that when it is time for them to vote, they will never again let someone like Trump become president.

* * *

The first part of this book brings together moving and eloquent essays by parents who are deeply frightened, angry, and sometimes despondent about the presidency of Donald Trump. Each parent has an important, often profound story to tell, a story that reveals their own reactions to Trump's presidency, the reactions of their children, and the various ways they have communicated with their children in the wake of the presidential election. Some of these stories remind us that racism has a long history in our country, and Trump is just our most recent bigoted example. Some express parents' fears that they and their children will never feel safe and secure again. Some parents worry that the democratic values we hold will be irrevocably harmed. But some express their hope that times can change and that they and their children will become agents of that change.

In this regard, the Trump presidency has had significant unintended consequences; we are seeing a more extensive and more powerful opposition to this president than ever before. This new groundswell of social activism is awakening people all over the country to stand up and be counted in the protest against Trump. (There is even a "Trump Regrets" Twitter account, which retweets statements of outrage and disappointment by those who voted for the president.) The groups Trump has targeted, including Muslims and Mexicans, are being supported by hundreds of thousands of Americans who are raising money for them, training to defend immigrants from deportation, creating safe sanctuary zones, and calling out the cowardice of their congressional representatives. If anything good emerges from these next years, it will be this unprecedented national response. The millions of women and men and children who have taken to the streets, the judges who have rallied to defeat the administration's unconstitutional orders, and the mayors and governors who have created and are protecting their sanctuary cities all demonstrate this unique call to social action. As parents, we hope our children will continue this civic commitment into the next generation.

In the second part of the book, I have tried to illustrate the ways in which an understanding of your child's ongoing development, the power of conversation, the contribution of narrative, and the commitment to action can help strengthen you and your child to master the social, emotional, and political challenges that lie ahead. I have been a clinical psychologist in practice for over four decades. My specialty is child and adolescent development, with a particular focus on helping parents talk to their children about difficult topics. (I've written a popular book on that subject as well.) Many of the issues raised by the Trump presidency are not new. Parents have always struggled to help their children in the face of bullying, lying, bigotry, and significant threats to their safety and well-being.

What *is* new in this country today is the fact that the bullying, lying, bigotry, and threats are emanating from and are endorsed by our highest governmental officials. This adds a whole new dimension to the task that parents face, making easy reassurances unrealistic for all but the youngest children. In this book, I have tried to offer topic-specific, age-appropriate advice for parents struggling with "How Do I Explain This to My Kids?" I hope parents of all sorts of children and teenagers will find this advice useful. I also hope it will let you know that you are not alone, encourage you to add your voice to ours, and help you to be the very best parent you can in the difficult Age of Trump.

HOW DO I EXPLAIN THIS TO MY KIDS?

Part One

How Do I Explain This to My Kids?

Here's What I'm Telling My Brown Son About Trump's America

Mira Jacob

Mira Jacob is the author of the critically acclaimed novel The Sleepwalker's Guide to Dancing. *She lives in New York.*

HERE IS WHAT I REMEMBER FROM THE TIME BEFORE WE EVER thought someone like Donald Trump could become an American president: I was twenty-eight, walking to work. On the corner of 11th Street and 7th Avenue, the traffic was sluggish. If I had looked past the windshields, I would have seen all the eyes turned to the sky. If I'd looked farther down the street, I would have seen all the people pouring into it. As it was, I looked to my side. Two teenage boys perched on a low wall by the hospital. One of them gestured down the avenue and I saw it, a smoking gash in one of the Twin Towers.

"New York City, man," the other said, and rolled his eyes the way we liked to back then, when we pretended even the worst things about the city couldn't surprise us because hadn't we seen it all?

I walked to a payphone and called your grandfather collect.

"A plane just flew into a building out here," I told him, imagining the Cessna he'd taught me to fly as a teenager in New Mexico.

Your grandfather came to America from India in 1968. From the start, he was in love with this country's modernity, its streamlined efficiency, the way everyone always seemed to be hurtling toward an impossibly bright future. He was always smiling at contrails. "This country," he'd say, "what a place!"

It was no Cessna, your grandfather told me on the phone that day. A few minutes later, when the second plane hit and everyone's cell phones went down, I began relaying news from his television set to the group who'd gathered around me. *Commercial airliners. Terrorist attack. People are jumping out of the buildings.*

A woman ran up the street, purse banging into her side. "Please! My husband is in tower two!"

I hung up and handed her the phone. I walked into the street with everyone else. Thirty seconds later, tower two fell.

Here is what I remember about that: falling with the building. Not knowing until my knees hit the road. Thinking to myself: *Get up. Do not fucking crawl in the middle of Seventh Avenue. No one crawls in the middle of Seventh Avenue unless they want to die.* But the ground was roaring into the palms of my hands louder than any subway could, and it felt like it was trying to tell me something. For months after that, I would find myself unable to breathe, cupping my hands over my ears. From the outside it probably looked like I was trying not to hear anything.

I was trying to hear everything.

When you were little, you asked me why I was brown.

"I'm Indian," I told you.

"From India?"

"Born here. My parents are Indian."

"Am I Indian?"

4

"You are half Indian."

"Am I half brown?"

"More or less."

"Because Daddy is Jewish and white-skinned so I am also half Jewish and half white-skinned."

"Exactly."

"But in the summer I turn brown like you are now."

"Yeah, true."

"And then YOU turn into a black person."

"Not exactly," I said.

You are eight years old now. When I tell you about things like this, you laugh like *oh brother* because you know better. You are a Brooklyn kid. You've seen some people.

This summer, as Donald Trump picked off his competition for the 2016 election, you learned to read the newspaper. You had more questions.

"Does Donald Trump hate all brown people?"

"Hate is a strong word."

"Does he not like brown people?"

"Some."

"Like Mexicans and Muslims?"

"Yes."

"What about brown boys like me? Does he not like brown boys like me?"

"What's not to like about you?" I asked. Then I grabbed you and tickled you and sank my face into your stomach, where you would not see my fear.

Here's what I know: On Sept. 12, 2001, America saw me for the first time. Until then, I'd been mostly innocuous—maybe a cabbie's daughter, maybe a television neurosurgeon, maybe a friend of the Patels. On the spectrum of American consciousness pre-9/11, South Asians lived somewhere between smart and smelly, and it seemed the worst thing we could be accused of was giving white men food poisoning.

Then we became the enemy. When I tell my Syrian Christian family back in India this, they cannot fathom it.

"But those fools were Saudi!" they say. "Muslims! Terrorists!"

"The white American imagination does not make those distinctions," I would have told them then, if I'd understood it myself. What I knew was less concrete, but just as disturbing: When it came to stripping us of our rights, most forms of harassment would be hidden under the benign umbrella of Better Safe Than Sorry.

At the airport, my father was pulled off a plane and questioned when two white women passengers found him suspicious. At separate ends of the country, my brother and I could not get through a single security line without being "randomly" searched. In the subway station, an older lady looked at me and my black backpack with so much fear I thought she might pass out on the tracks. When I turned and opened it so she could see my laptop, she screamed and ran back up the stairs.

We had it easy, compared to our Muslim and Sikh friends. We had no last names to atone for, no turban to explain, no mosques to protect, no need, in subsequent attacks, to throw pre-emptive apologies into the abyss of American fury. South Asians in America at that moment watched our Muslim and Sikh friends and worried, but with a slight beat of hesitation, a politeness I still regret. What happened in that moment? Did we simply not know how to quickly and forcefully mobilize, having never done it before? Did we worry that by protecting the rights of Muslims and Sikhs, we were aligning ourselves with their fate? Or am I flattering myself by believing our instant, united response would have made any difference?

Sometimes I wish I could ask America when, exactly, it made its mind up about us. The myth, of course, is that it hasn't, that there is still a chance to mollify those who dictate the terms of our experience here, and then be allowed to chase success unfettered by their paranoia. To live, as it's more commonly known, the American dream.

A lot of our couple friends broke up after Sept. 11, 2001. Your father and I had just moved in together the day before. We did not break up. Part of this was simple attraction. No one makes me laugh like your father does, no one interests me more, no one smells as good. But part of it, I know now, was a reaction to seeing our city fall apart. I am not talking about the buildings downtown, but what came after: the flags up in every window, the smug assurance that there was nothing to worry about if we had nothing to hide, the mourning of New York as a tarnished crown jewel instead of a multicultural mecca so many of us thrived in. The assumption this city was not also ours to lose.

Your father and I mourned the city together, and if before we'd had very little real thought about the symbolism of marrying outside of our race, now it became an act of defiance, a way to put faith in our better hearts. Five years after we married, we had you. Three weeks after that, Barack Obama was elected president. That night, we ran down the streets and laughed and cried and danced with our neighbors. You slept in a cocoon over my heart the whole time.

Here is the truth about us: Your father and I have been on different racial trajectories in this country for some time now. We do not always understand each other. But we always try. Some events are scarier than others. As white Americans justified the deaths of Trayvon Martin, Michael Brown, and Sandra Bland, we both felt horrified, but I was the one who fell into mute terror. Likewise, when we talked about it, I was the one who felt responsible—not for their deaths, exactly, but for my former belief in an America that did not exist for them, and further, for the melanin I'd dropped into your skin as your mother, for naming you after a Muslim musical hero of mine, for believing my child would be welcome and safe in this America.

Your father's parents are Republicans living in Florida. For years, this had led to the kind of dinner discussions we've all tried to avoid, with your father devolving into righteous incoherence as your grandmother cites Fox News references. But even though he falls far from the tree, your grandparents love your father dearly, and he loves them back. With you, they are gentle, funny, loving, and wise, which I think is maybe why you've been so confused as national events have played out. In the last few months, your questions have become particularly acute.

"Grandma and Grandpa are really voting for Trump?"

"Last I heard, yes."

"But aren't they scared that Trump is racist?"

"I don't think they think of him that way."

"So he's not racist?"

"No, he is, but . . . I think they don't really look at that part. They are voting for him for other reasons that make sense to them."

"But won't they be scared for us if he wins?"

"Your grandparents love you a lot."

"But what if—"

"A lot."

And then in bed that night, just when I thought you'd conked out, "But can't you just ask Grandma and Grandpa not to vote for Trump? Can't you say, please, you live in Florida, do it for us?"

I said no quickly and firmly and we had to read a whole other book just to get you to go to sleep. But that night, when you were sleeping, I typed up an email. *Dear Mom and Dad*, I wrote. I made the best case I could. *Please*, I wrote, *for us*. I cried as I wrote it. I read it three times to make sure it was the absolute best letter I was capable of writing. Then I deleted it because the only thing worse than having to beg them to imagine our lives would be hearing them say no.

I cannot take another no right now. I have lost people all my life to nos, and this year the pace upped significantly. A fan of my novel scolded me for writing about race, saying I had overstepped my place as a writer, as if she were the arbitrator of it. A colleague eager to prove himself on the "right side" of racism threw a tantrum and ended our acquaintance when I suggested my life looked different than his imagining of it. A good friend talking to me about the Black Lives Matter movement tried to explain how race in America really works, as if I do not live it, and then told me my thoughts were all in my head anyway, as if that is not generally the case with thoughts. All of these people were white. All of them felt galled by my not reassuring them of their goodness at every turn in the conversation. But the truth is, I have no more reassurance left for my white friends and family. I am saving it all for you.

Over the last week, you would ask me questions at bedtime and I would answer them, kiss you goodnight, and go to the bathroom to sit alone and shake.

"If Trump doesn't like boys who look like me, does that mean the government won't like me? The army? What about the police?"

I reminded you that we have two very nice police officers we see regularly on our block, that you have uncles and cousins in the military, that the government has many checks and balances. I told you that the likelihood of a Trump election was very low, that he had to get Florida to win at all, that he probably wouldn't.

The morning of the election, I woke up with so much in my heart, I was scared to move. I decided to wear a tuxedo to the polls. You and your father wore your own tuxedos in support. I marked my ballot, you put your hand on top of it, and we sent our prayer into the ballot box.

That night, we had an election party, and when the results started coming in, you grew very still on the couch. You watched with us as Florida grew tighter and tighter. As Wisconsin and Michigan went up for grabs. You watched me collapse into your father and then stand straight up again to take you to bed. In bed, you asked, "What if she doesn't win? What if the country doesn't like us anymore? What if they only like Daddy? Will he have to give us up?"

I told you it wasn't like that, that no one would let that happen. I told you we would be okay no matter what happened.

Out in the living room, after you went to sleep, people's armor started slipping. At one point, your many dark-skinned aunties and I had backed into the hallway while our white friends stared in disbelief at the television. One came over.

"Are you guys here because you feel like if you get away from the television, it can't happen?" He wasn't asking in a mean way, he was asking as a white man who has fathered two black children, who has been navigating huge swells of anxiety about America for decades. We nodded.

"Every poll that comes in, I think, they hate us. They hate us. You guys really fucking hate us," one of your aunties said, and started crying. He nodded and did not fight her and I loved him for that—for coming over to check in, for listening and standing with us, for understanding that his ego was the least important thing to protect in that moment.

We turned off the television at two a.m. At four, I bolted awake with a surge of fear I have not felt for fifteen years. The weight of it pushed the air out of my lungs. My phone buzzed. It was your Auntie Alison. Auntie Alison's parents are white and emigrated from working-class England. She is no more or less American than I am, but her skin color allows her a different perception. We talk about this all the time. She is my closest friend. She wrote: *Can't sleep. Just wanted to let you know I love you. I love your family.*

One hour later, you crawled into our bed. "Did she win?" you asked.

"No."

"What?"

"No, honey, she didn't."

"Trump won?"

"Yes."

"President Trump?"

"Yes."

At first I thought it was my body shaking, but then I realized it was yours. I curled myself around you.

"What will happen to us?"

"We will be okay. We will keep going."

"President *Trump*?"

"Oh, sweetie."

I told you that you and Daddy and I would be okay. I repeated that Martin Luther King Jr. quote I'd just seen on Instagram about the arc of the universe bending toward justice. I told you love was stronger than hate and that was an actual fact because if you ever watched super-hero movies, the guy who was fighting for love always beat the guy fighting for hate. We decided to watch action movies this weekend.

In the coming days, weeks, months, and years, some people will try to tell you this election was like any other, the same way they will try, when you are older, to tell you your experience of living in your own skin is "all in your head." This is nonsense. You will see me having no patience for this. Prepare to hear things like, "I do not believe this for a moment. It saddens me that you do." That will be my tamped down, eight-year-old-audience-appropriate version of what I'd rather say to them, which is, "I am a brown American woman who has been watching this country from its margins for forty-three years. There is nothing you can teach me about your normal that I don't already know and loathe."

Here is what I would tell you if you were older: This moment is like nothing else and like many things we have lived through before. It is the culmination of the last eighteen months, yes, but also the flesh and blood materialization of a shadow that dogged the entire Obama presidency, a by-product of the righteous anger we've nurtured since 9/11, and tangible evidence—as if we needed more—that America does not yet know how to love and value its people of color, its immigrants, its Muslims, its gays, its disabled, its women. It is a gash in a building that becomes a second gash in another building that becomes a rumbling that will send you to your knees on the street.

But listen, love, because I need to remind you of something and I need you to remember it extra well over the next four years: This is our street. *It is our street.* So when you feel that rumbling pushing up through your palms, I want you to press them flat against it, and do not be afraid to hear *everything.*

Hear what is falling all around us. Hear your innocence being taken as quickly as you turn a corner in your own city. Hear a country that has been rough on minorities since its inception, and will continue to be so now at an accelerated rate. Hear people ignoring this basic truth because it is convenient for them to do so. Hear your grandparents loving you and electing a man who does not, and know that though that is fraught, though it is complex, it does not make their love for you any less real. Know that you will still need this love, in all its complexity, that it is okay for you to give and receive it. Hear that these are the true corridors of the America you will have to navigate, the ones that might fill you with wonder one day, self-doubt and fury the next. Hear my phone ringing all day and night right now with friends of all backgrounds who say, "I love you. I will protect you and your family." Hear your father and me talking quietly in the next room as you sleep, trying to stay honest, alert, and kind even as we discuss our disappointments in this world, in each other. Hear us finding each other, again and again. Hear that this is what love in America can look like.

How Do I Explain to My Daughters What Happened in This Election?

Dan Kois

Dan Kois edits and writes for the culture department at Slate.

IN 1984 I WAS NINE, AND NO ONE REALLY TALKED TO ME ABOUT HOW polling worked in the days leading up to Election Day. Maybe there wasn't really that much polling—like, maybe *FiveThirtyEight* wasn't even a website yet? At any rate, I simply assumed that my parents' favored candidate, Walter Mondale—and his vice-presidential pick, Geraldine Ferraro—would win. And so when I woke up the morning after the election to see that in fact they had lost forty-nine of fifty states, I was crushed to realize that in fact most of America did not agree with my parents or with me.

I thought of 1984 on election night as the results started spiraling into nightmare-land. Our two daughters spent the summer cheering with us for Hillary Clinton. We made them sit through her entire convention speech; we talked to them about what it meant for a woman to assume the highest office in the land; we were honest with them about how Donald Trump thought and felt and spoke about women. We took them with us Tuesday morning to vote and posted optimistic photos to Facebook.

And then it was ten p.m., and things looked bad, bad, bad. As we walked home from our neighbors' house for a very late bedtime, both girls asked if Hillary was going to win. "It doesn't look good," I said. Harper, who's nine, wanted to nail down some specifics about red states and blue states, and which one our state, Virginia, had turned out to be. Lyra, who's eleven, was more blunt: "That horrible misogynist better not win."

Now it's two in the morning. Virginia is blue, and the horrible misogynist won. We've tried throughout this campaign to be honest with our kids about our hopes and dreams for this election, but tonight, on election night, I realized I never really found a way to be honest with them about our fears. In six hours they'll wake up and we'll have to figure out how to talk to them about the election; about the next few years; about what this means about how their country thinks not only of women but of queer people, immigrants, and people of color.

So what do we say? The natural inclination of a parent is to protect his kids. This is my instinct even as my children get old enough to begin to understand the world. What I want to tell them is that things will be fine, America is still the best, we'll have a chance to elect a woman four years from now. I want to hide our ashen faces and give them the long historical view and say: It's going to be OK.

That would be hard, if still easier than being honest. But maybe that's the wrong move. Not only because who the hell knows if everything's going to be OK. Maybe if we want to raise girls who are ready to fight for the better country they deserve, we need to wake them up tomorrow, the first day of a changed America, and break their hearts. We need to tell them the truth, even though the truth—half of America thinks so little of them that they were willing to elect a man who only cares how fuckable they will one day be—is scary and sad. (Maybe I won't use the word *fuckable*.)

I'm going to try. Am *I* strong enough? Beats me. (I can't even imagine how much more difficult this conversation will be for parents of color.) I don't know how hard it was for my parents to tell nine-year-old me in 1984 that Ronald Reagan won. But I bet they weren't surprised the way I have been tonight, thanks to whatever stone-age polling was tipping them off. This time around I'm conveying the full weight of my disappointment and apprehension to a couple of girls I failed to prepare for such a thing. I expect they'll remember it the rest of their lives. I hope so.

As a Muslim, How Do I Tell My Child the New President Doesn't Like Us?

Mehdi Hasan

Mehdi Hasan is an award-winning journalist and the presenter of Al Jazeera English's Head to Head *and* UpFront *based in Washington, D.C.*

"DID SHE WIN?" MY BLEARY-EYED NINE-YEAR-OLD HAD FALLEN ASLEEP on our couch the previous night, as the polls closed in Florida. When she sat across the breakfast table from me, I had to break the news that, while her own state of Virginia might have (narrowly) opted for Hillary Clinton, most of the other swing states—Ohio, Pennsylvania, Michigan—went with Donald Trump. "So we won't have a female president?" she asked, looking disconsolate.

I couldn't bring myself to tell her that she, we, minority communities across the board, had bigger problems to worry about. The normalization of racism, of antisemitism, of misogyny, but, above all else—in terms of the impact on her own life and future—Islamophobia.

How do I reveal to my Muslim daughter that women who look and dress like her mother have had their hijabs torn from their heads, as part of a wave of physical attacks on people of color since election day? Or that her fellow schoolkids aren't inoculated from this sort of violent hatred either? A Muslim high-school teacher in Georgia was left a note on her desk telling her to "hang" herself with her hijab, which "isn't allowed any more." The note was signed, "America."

How do I explain to my daughter, a proud U.S. citizen who recites the pledge of allegiance in class every morning, that millions of her fellow Americans elected as her next president a man who claims her faith "hates" America, and who falsely accused Muslim Americans of celebrating on 9/11 and of not reporting terrorists to the authorities? The FBI recently revealed that hate crimes against Muslims in the U.S. increased by 67% in 2015, to reach a level of attacks not seen since the aftermath of 9/11.

How do I share with her that one of Trump's signature policy plans was to prevent her grandparents, her cousins, her uncles and aunts—basically every single Muslim relative of hers living abroad—from entering the U.S. purely on the basis of their religion?

How do I break it to her that the "ban" isn't the only Trump proposal to brazenly discriminate against peaceful, law-abiding Muslims? That the president has also said that my daughter and other Muslim Americans have to be registered on a database and, when asked by a reporter how his proposal differed from the Nazi registry of German Jews, he replied: "You tell me."

How do I explain to her that the best way to identify a Trump supporter in the U.S., according to a recent study by Hamilton College political scientist Philip Klinkner, is to ask: "Just one simple question: is Barack Obama a Muslim?" Because "if they are white and the answer is yes," says Klinkner, "89 per cent of the time that person will have a higher opinion of Trump than Clinton," and it is more accurate than asking people their views on the economy or even if they are Republican.

How do I tell her about the Ku Klux Klan, a domestic U.S. hate group traditionally known for white nationalism and anti-black racism, but now recruiting new members "to fight the spread of Islam"? The KKK officially endorsed Trump's presidential bid while former Klan leader David Duke bragged that "our people" played a "huge role" in getting him elected to the Oval Office. Next month, an emboldened KKK is planning a pro-Trump celebration parade in North Carolina. How do I show her pictures of that?

I can't put it off much longer. At some stage soon I have to have the conversation with my daughter that all Muslim parents dread. The "Islamophobia conversation." The discussion in which you have to ask your child to be restrained, to be careful when they talk about their faith and their beliefs in public because, unbeknown to them, there are people out there who see them as a threat; who fear Muslims and loathe Islam.

How do I tell her that one of those people now includes her own president?

Parenting in the Shadow of Trump

John Culhane

John Culhane is the H. Albert Young Fellow in Constitutional Law at Delaware Law School and a frequent contributor to Slate, *where he writes the monthly column on parenting, "Hey, Daddy!"*

(Based on "How Should Parents Explain Donald Trump to Their Kids?" and "Don't Just Talk to Your Kids About Trump. Turn Them Into Activists," which originally appeared on *Slate*)

HOW MUCH SHOULD I TALK ABOUT POLITICS WITH MY JUST-turned-twelve-year-old twins? The question urgently demanded an answer during this past election season, and I'm still trying to work it all out now that the awful consequences are unfolding.

Early on, I thought that *politics* would mean the candidates' positions on various issues. But that was before it became clear the campaign would be largely issue-starved.

At some point during the campaign, I saw a Twitter post that stopped me in my tracks—a photograph of the back of someone's car, emblazoned with these two bumper stickers:

And there it was. The apotheosis of the anger, the violence, and the vitriol that stand as the tragic legacy of the horrifying campaign season. If any two images can carry the full freight of the culture war Trump has set ablaze, it's this pair. The Confederate battle flag isn't just for racists anymore. Now it also signals an angry male identity that lashes out at urban, millennial, educated elites. And who better to represent *that* bundle of despised stuff than the rainbow flag? All of those people might as well be gay. We *know* they're alien. Trump's mostly left LGBTQ people alone, but it hardly matters. The angriest partisans on the right are fully engaged, and they're not picky about the specific targets.

What could I, a gay dad, possibly tell my kids about all this—an election in which much of the national sentiment can be summed up in one figure kicking another in the gut? My husband and I let them watch one of the debates with us and two other couples. I looked on in despair as the six children—all girls, ages eleven to sixteen—had to witness the dark sludge oozing through the screen. I conveniently remembered it was a school night and shooed our kids to bed about halfway through.

They didn't ask questions about any of it the next day, and I was grateful for that. I tried to pry something out of them (and from their friends) about how they viewed the election and Trump. Mostly, they were mum. But one Sunday, driving with a couple of their friends back from their birthday party weekend, one of my daughters asked if we'd move to Canada if Trump won. Apparently, this possibility was discussed at school. I found myself saying "maybe"—and, for the first time, almost meaning it.

The problems are only more acute now that Trump has gained the presidency. The dogs of war have been slipped, and the violence has bubbled up on both sides. This began before the election. In North Carolina—lately ground zero in the culture war—a GOP headquarters was firebombed by unknown, angry activists. A graffito on a nearby building demanded that "Nazi Republicans Leave Town Or Else." The retaliatory ugliness is predictable, scary, and not easy to tamp down once unchained.

For instance, the ugly bumper sticker depicted on the opposite page led to a "counter-sticker" Confederate versus Rainbow image: This one showed the tables turned, with the Rainbow Avenger kicking the Confederate Creep right in that same, sensitive spot. This is what we've come to, and the early signs are that the president isn't softening his tough-guy persona now that he's in office. If anything, his thinly disguised ban on Muslim refugees is a clear sign that things are now worse. To cite another example, an early budget draft contemplates eliminating grants to states to fund initiatives related to violence against women. And, among many other initiatives, his administration has taken down all reference to the LGBTQ community from the POTUS website.

I've thought a lot about how to introduce these deeper concerns about divisiveness and ruinous policy with the kids. Getting them to understand how divided and how angry our political leaders and the broader society have become is a big part of any conversation about the underlying issues these days. It's not enough to understand that climate change is real, and what's likely to happen—they also need to know how sclerotic and obstructionist Congress has become. ("Sclerotic" will also be a useful vocabulary-builder.) And the Senate's indefensible refusal to consider Supreme Court nominees—which we must not allow ourselves to forget—has to be part of any conversation about why the Court's membership matters so much. (Even twelve-year-olds know that eight is a bad number for a court; when I asked what they thought of a nine-member court minus one, they said: "But what if there's a tie?")

The harder thing to explain is the *why* of all this divisiveness. How can I connect the dots for them from these points: congressional obstructionism; Trump's success in using a racist, xenophobic attack on the president's citizenship to launch his vile political career; and the explosive hatred that's gotten almost impossible to avoid?

After the election, I did feel the need to have "the talk" with them about what a Trump presidency bodes. But now I'm sick of talking. I'm a law professor and a columnist: *All I do* is talk, and write. If the results of the election told us anything, it's that talking isn't enough. Has so much carbon dioxide ever been spewed in the service of so little substance? I'm reminded of the casual brilliance of the Staple Singers, who decades ago floated a simple strategy for a healthier environment: "Put your hand over your mouth when you cough—that'll help the solution."

At some point, who cares what any of us say? A conversation about how important it is to protect those in more vulnerable positions than our family's now sounds to me as a kind of self-congratulation. Easy, but of limited value, like the well-intentioned safety pin that was briefly the fashion accessory *de rigueur* after November 8. Worse, talking without doing sends exactly the wrong signal, given the stakes—especially to our kids.

So, at the end of my talk, I discussed with them the importance of activism. And that's what we need to do: not just explain things to our children, but shepherd them toward a life of activism. Since we live in Philadelphia—where more than a quarter of the residents live in poverty, and homelessness is a constant—a couple of obvious acts of practical kindness occurred to our girls.

"If we're going to be walking around later today, why don't we bring some water bottles and food to give to homeless people?"

"Don't we have clothes we can give away? We never even wear some of them."

This kind of buy-in makes it easier to get them interested in next steps. Our family is already invested in what will soon be a community-wide commitment to activism. Shortly after the election, we met with like-minded neighbors to discuss what we can do. We've begun to sort out issues and potential partners, and to think about what actions we might want to take. My children attended an event designed to get kids to understand and commit to social and economic justice from an early age.

The inspiration for this nascent collective was formed in the brain of a millennial neighbor, who is the program coordinator for Al-Bustan, an organization that, per its website, is "dedicated to presenting and teaching Arab culture through the arts and language." We developed our initial plan together, through Facebook and follow-up emails to every local we could think of who might be interested, and the idea for a meeting of neighborhood friends—who, until now, have mostly gotten together to drink, or, as in this case, to complain about current events that don't go our way—soon blossomed into this more comprehensive plan.

Tough issues are still being hammered out, and at this point it's not even clear to me what kinds of ideas and initiatives might emerge. The recent March on Washington, though, energized everyone. Many people in our neighborhood group attended. Our family contributed to the ranks of our local Philadelphia event instead. To start, some of us might want to get involved in local politics, which can stand piles of improvement in the city. The entrenched Democratic leadership has gotten entirely too complacent, and the party machine is about to grind to a halt. Maybe some of us can help provide a jolt.

Boring down to the most local level, our Powelton Village community, a formerly motley polyglot of quasi-hippies that's now gelled into a harder-to-define assortment of professionals, artists and artisans, and academics, has been discussing how we can join forces with Mantua, the predominantly African-American neighborhood to our immediate north. It won't be easy, because there are grievances and tensions between the two communities that go back a long way. We might also want to involve local Drexel University, which lately has been a robust partner to both communities.

This commitment to activism presents challenges to my family. Most of what my kids like, and what feels the most useful to them are actions that have an immediate, observable effect. My few skills really are centered around writing and speaking, with organizing a distant third. So I'll doubtless find myself doing things with my daughters that aren't the most effective use of my limited time and skills.

Yet there will be some things that we can do as a family. We can register voters, going door-to-door. We can do mailings. Most important, we can listen and learn from each other, and from the community we're a part of.

The quest to understand what went wrong will continue, and it's important to get all the facts and analysis we can. But in the end, what can really make a difference is organizing for social change.

This won't be easy. I'll confess that until the post-inauguration protest events, I was having trouble moving through the despair. I was struck by an artist's rendering of her deepest fear in a visual op-ed that ran in the Sunday's *New York Times* shortly after the election. Cynthia Kittler's work depicted a head, stony and scarred, lying on a bed and staring at the ceiling. The caption read: "I might become a passive stone that escapes in thinking instead of taking action." Marching can do more good than we often realize, because it reminds folks that it's time to get out of that bed and do something. As Shakespeare knew, "Joy's soul lies in the doing," after all.

"Only White People," Said the Little Girl

Topher Sanders

Topher Sanders covers race and inequality at ProPublica. He lives in Maplewood, New Jersey.

FEW THINGS ARE MORE AWESOME THAN LISTENING TO KIDS PLAYING on the playground. There's magic in that mix of laughter and exhausted breaths—giggle, pant, giggle.

Just the other Saturday at Maplewood's Memorial Park, I was watching my five-year-old playing with his friends from day care. The kids have just started kindergarten and are now split up among four schools. Some industrious mom had the idea to get them together again.

It was a great idea. It was also the moment when I saw the messy birth of my son's otherness.

They were playing on one of those spinning things—you know, the one where kids learn about centrifugal force and as a bonus get crazy dizzy. They were having a blast.

"Only white people," said a little girl.

I heard it, but I wasn't quite sure that's what I heard.

"Not you, you're black," said the girl, reaching out to touch my son. "You're not white. Only white people can play."

What to do? How to do it? What to say? How to say it?

I couldn't escape the searing historical parallels of a little white girl telling a little black boy—my son—what he can and cannot do because of his skin color.

My instinct was to go over and drop science on her and all of the other little children.

But then my systems kicked in. My automatic scary-black-man recalibration systems. The infinitesimal adjustments that black men employ not only to succeed in school and at work, but also to help us keep it 100, stay woke, all while trying to make white folks feel comfortable enough to keep us around.

Whether it's turning down your Kendrick Lamar when the white woman gets on the elevator or flashing those disarming smiles at white women you pass at night on the sidewalk, black men learn to present safeness.

Why do I always have to make white people feel comfortable at the expense of who I am and my mood and my music and my thoughts?

Walter Scott—and every other unarmed black man killed by police officers—is why.

To support a family is why.

If I scared the white people at the playground with my reaction, what would be the impact on our little family in Maplewood? Would we be on the next email thread for a play date? Would the other families talk about my son's angry dad?

I made all these calculations in the five seconds after he was told he couldn't play because he was black.

Then I noticed my son. When the little racist girl reached out to touch him, he moved out of the way and laughed. He kept right on playing.

The garbage that came out of that child's mouth meant nothing to him. Yet. It marks the beginning of what is likely to be a gradual process. One day he'll wonder why, when he plays with a certain group of friends, he is always the villain. Similar inquiries will follow, until he has his own system of recalibrations and adjustments.

I knew a moment like this would happen eventually. I just didn't think it would happen at age five on the playground.

And what of the little girl? She, too, is a casualty in this—infected by racism before she can even spell the word.

It would be easy to dismiss the whole exchange as kids being kids. She's young enough that she hasn't developed the filters to catch what she's being taught at home. There's a direct line from what she's learning to her mouth. I thought about all the time my son spent with this child in his day care class. What else had she expressed to him, or to the other students about him?

Besides the idea that, just by virtue of her complexion, she is more entitled to something as simple as spinning on the playground.

Who will she become when she grows up? Will she be a prosecutor, a manager at a tech firm, a politician? Systemic racism apparently begins at the playground.

I was still processing the incident while my son and his friends ran over to the slides.

I turned to the parent closest to me, who hadn't heard the exchange. "Who is that child?" I asked.

The dad told me the girl's name and pointed out her mother. The mom was standing about a dozen feet away in a group of other moms talking about how the kids were adjusting to kindergarten.

I tried to imagine a productive confrontation, but couldn't get beyond my opening line: "Excuse me, can we talk about the racist trash that just came out of your daughter's mouth?"

I told the dad next to me what had happened. He didn't know what to say, because honestly, who really does? He unfortunately did what a lot of white people do in these moments: He tried to explain it.

"Really?" he said. "That's not her personality."

In the end I did nothing.

I agonized over it, of course. My wife and I have since had several discussions about what we could have done, what should have been said, and to whom. At one point I decided that the thing to do would have been to bring the matter directly to the parent. But leaving the children out of it didn't seem right.

I recalled a moment from my childhood in Hawaii. One of my best friends, Dominic, was white. He was from a big family and being at his house was like stepping into an '80s sitcom. I was over there all the time. Dominic's dad was my mom's boss on the Air Force base.

But one day, when I asked my mother if I could go to Dominic's, she said no. She said the same thing the next time I asked, and the next. After a few weeks, I gave up.

It wasn't until I was an adult that I heard the story. Dominic's family was having a party. We kids were probably in front of the Nintendo or running around the yard. The parents were inside, talking about the New York Knicks' full name, the Knickerbockers. "Their real name should be the New York Nigger-bockers," Dominic's mom said, with a laugh.

My mother, the only black person at the party, gathered her things, found me and told me it was time to go.

I don't blame my mother for not explaining. But I would have benefited from knowing what had happened.

Two years later, my mother and I moved to Montgomery, Ala. I walked into the halls of Alabama's public schools completely unprepared for the racial dynamics that would meet me there. It was an intense couple of years as I received a middle-schooler's crash course in racial truths.

Sitting here today, with the string of black men dying on camera at the hands of government agents who are often not held accountable, and with a major presidential candidate who passively, if not whole-heartedly, accepts the admiration of the KKK and other white suprem-acist groups, I must make a different decision from my mother.

My son has watched too many boys and men that look like him die before his eyes on television. We don't shield him from those images.

"What happened, Daddy?"

I explain.

"What did he do wrong?"

His mother and I exchange looks. I try to answer. Best I can. He pauses, then he's back to his Hot Wheels races.

So as I mulled how I could have handled the incident at the play-ground and how I will handle it the next time—because, sadly, there will be a next time—I rejected the idea of simply talking to the parents.

Instead I will interrupt the children as they play, or study, or swim in the pool. I will do this for three reasons.

First, the children being groomed to be racist need to learn that act-ing on their racism has consequences, the least of which is that they will be met with resistance. The children have to see that people will stand up to them and call out their ignorance.

Second, all the white children in earshot also need to see that resis-tance and be taught that standing by silently is an endorsement.

And most important, I have to model for my children ways for them to confront racism without going all scorched earth. They need to see from their parents how to speak to ignorance, wield their dignity and push back against individual and systematic efforts to define, limit and exclude them.

During the walk home from the playground, my wife, my son and I talked about race while our two-year-old daughter listened from her stroller.

My son nodded and said, "Yes, sir," the way a five-year-old does. It wasn't our first conversation on the subject. My wife and I have been very deliberate in our attempt to introduce him to concepts of race and history. The goal is for him to be confident, keen, yet still open-minded about those around him—a goal many adults are still striving for.

It's clear that someone in that little girl's life is pursuing a different goal.

We don't have a choice but to talk to our son about Ferguson, Eric Garner, workplace frictions, Baltimore, Charlotte, Alton Sterling and on and on. And yet I mourn each of those conversations. With each degree of awareness comes a corresponding loss—of silliness, of whimsy, of childhood.

How Kids Talk About Donald Trump

Molly Knefel

Molly Knefel is a writer, educator, and co-host of Radio Dispatch *based in New York.*

I PLAY A GAME WITH MY MIDDLE SCHOOL STUDENTS CALLED "MAKE IT Worse." It's meant to teach them about how making a good story is all about raising the stakes. I teach theater, and I use the game to try to counteract the kids' urge to create awesome characters with awesome lives who are good at everything. This particular class, at an after-school program in the Bronx, is made up of mostly bilingual Spanish and English speaking kids, with a few English language learners, and the kids translate for each other and for me as we go.

In February, we stood in a circle and took turns suggesting imaginary problems and piling onto them. "The problem is: El Chapo is at the park," said one of the kids in Spanish. All the others burst out laughing.

"That's a big problem," I said. "What else could happen that's even worse?"

"Donald Trump is also there," said the next kid. Everyone laughed even harder.

"What's even worse than that?" We continued in Spanish and English, with me, the only monolingual English speaker in the room, laughing on a delay.

"Donald Trump and El Chapo decide to work together to make it harder for immigrants to come into the country." I told them they are very good at this game.

Most of my students are either immigrants or children of immigrants. The majority are Latin American, some are Muslims, some from the Middle East, and some from West Africa. The youngest are kindergarteners and the oldest are eighth graders. And all year, they've been talking about Trump.

The first time I heard a kid mention him was in the first or second week of school. I was with a class of second graders playing a "get to know you" activity, and a girl said that her favorite food was tacos.

"Tacos are Mexican food," said the little boy next to me. A stream-of-consciousness monologue—classic seven-year-old style—followed. "I don't like Mexican food. It's from Mexico. I don't want Donald Trump to win. I don't want to have to go back to Santo Domingo."

The word association couldn't have been clearer: Mexican, Trump, deportation. Back then, in September, the mainstream consensus was still optimistically stuck on "Trump's bid for presidency is a funny joke that's going on a little too long." This was the moment I realized it wasn't a joke.

Children are, of course, political beings. They are humans who live in the world, and politics affect them. They observe, they watch, they listen, they pick up on more than we think they do, and they echo. The amount of people under the age of ten who've complained about taxes to me is surprisingly high. But I've never before had the experience of watching kids between the ages of five and fourteen engage so deeply not only with a politician, but with his proposed policies. It's not that they know about him—they knew Romney was running against Obama in 2012, but that was basically where the conversation started and stopped—but that they know exactly what he's saying.

They know what he's saying because Donald Trump doesn't speak in policy proposals. He speaks in threats that a seven-year-old can understand. Trump has the twelve-year-olds in my classroom joking about immigration policy. And while my students' jokes come from a shared perspective, Trump's hateful language can also be levied against kids from the same marginalized groups Trump is targeting. New York City education officials are afraid to hold mock elections in schools because it could lead to bullying. "Unless this is done right, this could be something else that is going to create more contention," schools Chancellor Carmen Fariña said in March.

Fariña didn't explicitly say whether it's Trump's xenophobic language or his general inter-personal cruelty that she's worried will inspire bullying. But if it's the former, her fears aren't unfounded. White students across the country have parroted Trump to harass kids of color. In Indiana, high schoolers at a basketball game held up a giant photo of Trump and chanted "Build a Wall" at the opposing team, whose students are majority Latino. At another high school basketball game in Iowa, students at a mostly white school chanted "Trump" during a game against a school that is about half kids of color, according to their coach, but whose team didn't even have any Latinos. And a Facebook post from the mother of a third grader in Virginia went viral after she described how the children were quoting Trump to bully one another:

> I just got a call from my son's teacher giving me a heads up that two of his classmates decided to point out the "immigrants" in the class who would be sent "home" when

Trump becomes president. They singled him out and were pointing and laughing at him as one who would have to leave because of the color of his skin. In third grade ... in Fairfax County ... in 2016!*

Meanwhile much of the commentary about Trump's effect on children has focused on his childish bullying tactics instead of his racism. Writing in *The Atlantic* former teacher Cynthia Leonor Garza argued: "Trump is an uncomfortable reminder that bullying isn't something people leave behind after high school." The author wondered what kind of example Trump's name-calling and physical threats send to her six-year-old daughter.

Garza is right to question the conventional characterization of bullying as a "kid problem" that originates in childhood and sometimes lingers a little too long into the grown-up world. But she downplays Trump's viciousness by focusing on his immature taunts. In fact it's Trump's bigotry that is the most blatant and dangerous form of bullying. Garza lumps together Trump's name-calling with his racism and xenophobia: "He calls [his opponents] stupid, losers, and rapists, belittles them with names like 'Little Marco,' and says he wishes he could punch them in the face." But if bullying often manifests in the interpersonal—calling Rubio names—it is the structural—calling Mexican immigrants rapists—that shows where the roots of all bullying really come from.

Attacking people for their perceived weaknesses is the name of the game in a capitalist system built on the illusion of meritocracy. Bullies of all ages target people who are too feminine or too masculine, too big or too small, too gay or too black or too poor or too different.

---

* Petula Dvorak, "The 'Trump Effect' Is Contaminating Our Kids—and Could Resonate for Years," *Washington Post*, March 7, 2016.

They target those who aren't properly conformed to white supremacy, to capitalism, to patriarchy.

The disconnect in how adults talk about bullying is perfectly embodied in Trump. While adults are worried about how his calling Rubio "Little Marco" sets a bad example for the children, kids across the country are pointing to their classmates in headscarves and their classmates speaking Spanish and saying, "Donald Trump will send you away."

At the middle school, the kids are writing a play together that they'll perform for their parents at the end of the year. It's about what they would do if there was a zombie apocalypse, and the first scene takes place at Starbucks, because one boy said that you need caffeine to fight zombies. I asked them to decide who else is in line at Starbucks, and they suggested Donald Trump (these same kids have a running joke that Starbucks is where white people go).

As a theater teacher, I've seen kids make plays about police violence, robbery, homelessness, overworked parents, subway dancers, pop stars, superheroes, vampires, and zombies. They act out their realities and their fantasies, their anxieties and their aspirations.

This year, they're making a play where they sacrifice Donald Trump to the zombie apocalypse. In the final line of that scene, all the kids scream, "Bye, Trump!"

The day after the election, I went into the school building bracing myself for how to talk to young people about what had just happened. One's natural instinct around kids who are scared is to comfort them, to tell them it will be okay. Before I could figure out how to do that, a student put his hand on my shoulder to reassure me. "Don't worry, Miss," he said. "I'm a citizen."

Donald Trump still has children discussing immigration policy in the cafeterias and gymnasiums of schools across the country. Since the election, educators have been in crisis management mode. After Trump implemented the Muslim ban, there were reports of students refusing to go to school out of fear that their parents wouldn't be there when they got home. Teachers are helping students through emotional breakdowns over their family's immigration status. What Donald Trump is doing to young people right now feels like emotional terrorism. The conversations I've had with young people since the election are specific: the girls fear the way he talks about women, the black children fear the way he talks about black people, the Latino children fear the way he talks about Latinos. But what makes those fears worse, to me, is how they are compounded by a child's imagination. Adults who follow politics for a living can't even predict how bad things could get under Trump—what about a ten-year-old who has less experience and less context and even less power over their own life?

Adults now, more than ever, must create an environment at school that actively affirms the humanity of all children. Viral photos have circulated of classroom doors with signs, written in magic markers, welcoming immigrants and refugees and affirming that black lives matter. For every population that Trump targets, he is targeting children. It's not just legal and political sanctuaries we need to fight for, but emotional ones too.

Can the Muslim American Family Survive Trump?

Huda Al-Marashi

Huda Al-Marashi's work has appeared in the Washington Post,
the LA Times, Al Jazeera, Refinery29, *and elsewhere. She lives
in Monterey.*

THE DAY AFTER THE PRESIDENTIAL ELECTION, MY FOURTEEN-YEAR-
old son left a message in the shower. With his little brother's foam
alphabet letters, he spelled out, "Haters gonna hate us."

It was the "us" that transformed the popular catchphrase into something troubling. I knew that the rhetoric of this election cycle had
affected my children, but here it was spelled out so clearly. My son felt
the vitriol towards Muslims directed at him.

Over the course of the week, my daughter would ask if we were going
to be banned from the country, pleading after my every reassurance,
"But how do you know?" My five-year-old son asked if Trump would
break our family. When I answered that as president, Trump would
learn to be nice, he ran to share this news with his older siblings, his
little feet light with relief.

I thought I faced discrimination when I was growing up as the daughter of Iraqi immigrants in a California seaside town. I still remember the first Gulf War and the novelty shops filled with distorted Arab faces on mugs and T-shirts, the camel jockey jokes, and the boy at the mall who told me to go back to Kuwait where I came from. Now I look back on the stereotypes and prejudice of the day, and it seems so innocent, so benign in comparison.

When I was in the eighth grade, my teacher was an all-American, white male who played baseball and never failed to remind us that the United States was the greatest country in the world, the one place where anyone can become anything. "It doesn't matter where you came from," he'd say, "America is a melting pot."

Although the melting pot analogy is dated and contentious, as a first-generation American and the only Muslim in a Catholic grade school, it meant something to have the person of authority in my classroom repeat that I not only belonged in this country, but that my story was somehow an intrinsic part of our nation's identity. "We're all immigrants," he'd say and look over at me. "Everyone here came from somewhere and that's exactly what makes America special."

At the time, his words hardly impressed me. I didn't need my teacher to tell me what I lived every day. My family home was overcrowded with immigrating relatives who had waited close to ten years for green cards to come to the U.S., and I knew the lived experience of immigration was far more complicated than this story of America's unbridled acceptance.

Melting pot or not, people were suspicious of my family's accents and our religion. My grandparents struggled to learn English and lived a life of relative isolation.

My classmates' curiosity, although mostly gentle and respectful, often made me feel like a foreign coin in their wallet, a token representation of all that was different. But I never doubted my right to be an American. Somewhere my teacher's message of equality had taken root within me.

I can't help but wonder if my children will grow up with a similar sense of security regarding their place in their country.

Last summer, our current president claimed that Muslims don't assimilate. In response to Sean Hannity's question about how to vet the hearts of Muslims coming to the U.S., Donald Trump replied, "Assimilation has been very hard. It's almost, I won't say nonexistent, but it gets to be pretty close. And I'm talking about second and third generation—for some reason there's no real assimilation."

I never thought I'd long for the most simplistic and contested views of immigration. I want the myth of our soupy integrated society to be an option once again, a goal. I want recognition for all the painful and inadvertent ways my family and I surrendered our heritage to our English-loving tongues and our western educations.

I tell my son about the melting pot myth I grew up with and ask him if he feels the U.S. can still call itself that. "Maybe for some people," he says, "but right now, it's like there's one ingredient that's giving everyone a rash and everybody just wants to pluck it out."

I'm glad my young son does not yet see the bitter irony of his statement. Terrorist activity caused America's allergy to Muslims, but it is exactly this physical rejection that terrorist groups have looked to exploit.

The Islamic State of Iraq and the Levant (ISIL) group has expressed its desire to eliminate the grey zone—the spaces inhabited by Muslims and non-Muslims alike, and our president is fully cooperating with their vision by suggesting Muslims in the U.S. are a fifth column.

This is the scenario I feared most after 9/11. My mind went straight to the hate. I saw it rippling through generations, the way it had with so many minority groups that had been forced to carry the blame for world events. Exactly a year after 9/11, my oldest son was born. It pained me to think he'd never know a time in this country when Muslims were not the enemy.

It is this generation of Muslim-Americans that weighs heavily on my mind. How will these smart, talented, vibrant young people maintain a sense of pride in their faith when their president rose to power on the promise of registering them in a database?

Political rhetoric matters. It filters down through our televisions, computers, and smartphones and straight into our bodies, shaping our self-concept and our attitudes towards others.

It is just as dangerous and lethal as any weapon in a government's arsenal. I hope, over the next four years, that Trump will choose his words more carefully.

Arm Them with Facts: Raising My Girls in Gainesville, Florida

Darlena Cunha

Darlena Cunha is a journalism professor at the University of Florida.

WE'VE LIVED AN ORDINARY LIFE, MY FAMILY AND I. MY TWIN DAUGHTERS are eight years old now, too young to remember the financial crash that devastated their parents and the nation at large. Too young to remember the elections we held where we overwhelmingly voted in a black president running on the platforms of hope and change.

They've never been political. They've never had to be. White privilege, in part, has shielded my twins from politics. In addition, I've kept my work as a writer at a distance from their multiplication homework and their reading comprehension tests. During the campaign, I amped them up about Hillary Clinton because she was a woman, but also because she was so well qualified to lead our country. I never spent much time on Trump. They knew the basics: a wall blocking Mexico, a ban based on religion, guns, sick people getting sicker with no help. I chopped up these little lessons into third-grade sound bites, so that they would understand what was going on, but not be bothered by it.

I was wrong.

When my kids caught me crying as I tried to ready them for school on November 9, they were unprepared for the news of our new president. They hadn't thought it a possibility. And living in Florida, it became my job to arm them with facts as they faced their celebrating schoolmates and teachers in the coming months.

Right after the election, their statements were incredulous, but upbeat.

"Bailey said Hillary has been in jail three times," one piped up on a ride home from school.

"And my teacher said Trump is a good man, and he got the most votes, so everyone needs to get over it!" the other one chimed in.

At first, I told them to avoid talking about it in school. I didn't want them to go to their Trump-leaning elementary school with targets on their backs for talking about all the reasons Trump should not have been elected. I was suddenly afraid of free speech. But I faced these by explaining the truth and showing them the context of the political world as we now know it, bit by bit. As time has gone by, their voices have lost that childish pep when talking about their schoolyard political disagreements.

When my daughter's teacher had them watch the inauguration, peppered with her comments about how great Trump was going to make America, she looked at me solemnly before quietly saying, "Don't worry, mommy, I didn't cry. I only let one tear fall. And I told them when they were wrong, but I didn't push it. They said that was just my opinion, but I know the truth."

They've seen me cry several times since election day, and at first my best explanation was simply, "Because Trump is president." Unsaid was that I cry because a man who treats women so much like trash is now our leader. I cry because legal residents of this country are being hunted down as if they're criminals. Because millions may no longer be able to see a doctor or afford medicine when they're sick. Because our leader is a racist and is pursuing policies that harm people of color in the United States. Because our president has surrounded himself with sycophants and eschewed our nation's long history of bipartisan councils and committees on everything from intelligence to security. How can you put all that into words? How can you look your children in their eyes and lay out their bleak future before them?

I decided I had to try.

I can't protect them any longer. Or rather, I protect them better by exposing them to the reality of our new administration. I had always worked to spare them from my political agenda, and, truth be told, during the W. Bush and Obama years, I'd never had much of an agenda. I was a passive citizen, allowing legislation to fly by me with little more than a gripe on social media.

No more. When I go to organizational meetings, I bring them and let them watch how true citizens and residents of the United States wield their power. When I call Senator Marco Rubio, I let them listen to my complaints. Before this election, I had never called my congresspeople. Now I do so every day, and my daughters' eyes and ears are on me. When the women marched on Washington, my kids and I marched together here in Gainesville, braving the middle fingers and blaring pickup trucks swerving toward the sidewalk to scare us.

My twins took the bullhorn and led the chants. I let them because they are the future, and they are the hope. They are the redemption for this country. They are the voters who will make change.

I let them because I want them to see that this is what democracy looks like.

They are what democracy looks like.

Making Kids Feel Safe in a Trump World Isn't Easy

Kera Bolonik

Kera Bolonik is the executive editor of DAME *Magazine. She lives in New York.*

THIS SUMMER, THE CLINTON CAMPAIGN RELEASED AN AD CALLED "Role Models" in which wide-eyed kids watched some of Donald Trump's most appalling moments: calling Mexicans "rapists," mocking a disabled reporter, longing for the good old days when protesters would be beaten. The ad gave parents a glimpse of what a Trump presidency might be like, but nothing could have prepared them for how to explain to their children what happened in the wee hours of November 9. How do you tell a kid who's excited about Hillary Clinton that the other guy won—especially when you're still trying to wrap your own mind around the news?

Latham Thomas, who is black, took her thirteen-year-old son to Hillary Clinton's Election Night party at the Javits Center in hopes of celebrating the breaking of the ultimate glass ceiling. But by nine p.m., she said, the mood went from joyous to ominous. "My son wanted to go," she says. "We left by around midnight. He was like, 'I don't want to cry out here, because, how is this our reality?' He only knows President Obama. I took him to Obama's inauguration when he was in kindergarten."

Thomas's son asked if he could take Wednesday off from school. "I thought he wanted to avoid gloating classmates," she said. But he clarified that he felt drained seeing everyone so sad at the party and knowing "'We were going to wake up to realize we're stuck with a bad guy.' And I do feel like we need to talk to our kids and give them the space to speak. This election was so nasty and so prominent—it was in the media and social media, and the kids were exposed to everything."

She decided to compromise with her son and let him sleep in, waking him up to watch Hillary Clinton's concession speech so they could discuss it afterward. "And then I took him to school. I assured him it would be a short day, but felt it was important he go. I said, 'We are going to get up and do what we have to do and we're not going to not be who we are. But I don't want you to hold on to feelings.' I just don't want him to let somebody make him change who he is or alter his peace of mind."

Thomas worries for her son, who, at age thirteen, is not finished growing. "As he gets older, the same people who say my black son is cute now will be trying to put him in jail because they will find him threatening." And with Trump at the helm, and the appointment of Jefferson Beauregard Sessions III as Attorney General—a man regarded as being too racist by the Senate Judiciary Committee to be appointed to the federal judiciary thirty years ago—that anxiety only intensifies.

Linda Villarosa, who lives in Brooklyn with her partner and high-school-age son (she also has a daughter away in college), watched the returns with her family. By night's end, "Nic, our very woke seventeen-year-old, was curled in my arms, crying—all six-foot-two of him," she says. "We had just gotten off the phone with his grandmother. Through my mother's sobs, she said she felt like all of the struggle she had been through as an eighty-six-year-old black woman in America had been erased. Nic was nine when President Obama was elected, came of age at a time of political idealism and social change, so his world was shattered."

But by Wednesday afternoon, Nic was transforming his grief into action. "He texted me from school and asked if he could attend the rally against Trump in Union Square," Villarosa says proudly. "I said yes, of course, and I'm going with him."

Jasmine Banks, a licensed therapist in Arkansas, says it's important to validate your kids' feelings. "When they say, 'I think Trump hates black people so much that he's gonna come kill all of us,' don't detract from the reality that this has happened around the world, but also remind them you're their parents and it's your job to keep them safe. Remind them you love them very much."

Banks currently lives in a "former sundown town" (i.e., forty years ago there was a sign that read "Niggers Not Out Past Dark") with her genderqueer partner, Mo, and three kids ages nine, six, and five. She says that "we allow our kids to feel the fear and reflect back what they're feeling, like, 'Oh, buddy, that sounds very scary, you're very scared right now, you're feeling a lot of anger.'" They prepared their children for the prospect of a Trump presidency because "they are black children and so they have a full understanding of what our future can look like when people in power who support white supremacy have the reins for things."

Her nine-year-old son had a mock election at school, and Trump won handily. "Most of his friends said Hillary wanted to kill babies in their mommies' belly, she wanted to let people be gay, and she was going to let Mexicans come and take over America," says Banks, "so we had a lot of ground to cover."

Still, no amount of preparation can quell the anxiety. "My oldest's first question was whether my partner and I, who are engaged, can still get married in May. What a difficult question for a child to ask," says Banks. "I explained it's gonna take a while for Trump to be able to make any changes to laws that have been established. But I didn't want to get in the trenches about it all, I just wanted to honor that that's where he was at and that's how he saw it."

"I think it's really important for folks to recognize that the wound on the collective psyche of children in the U.S. is going to be a deep and lasting one," she went on, "particularly for those of us on the margins, because our kids don't see this as a moment where a person just hates the collective Muslim identity, or the collective black identity. They look for the things that they identify within the people who keep them safe—their moms and dads and caregivers. They personalize it because that's where they're at in the world. They see a president who hates their mom."

Sara Duyal (not her real name), a divorced mother with two daughters, ages eight and ten, is surrounded by Trump supporters—not only her New Jersey neighbors, but her Turkish-Muslim parents and her ex-in-laws. "My parents accused me of brainwashing my daughters toward Hillary. It's been an awful ride. They believe in nationalism taken to almost a religious fervor. They will try to couch it in feminist terms, like Islamophobia is understandable because of terrorism and because Islam oppresses women. But there's no feminism involved beyond the ripping off of hijab. My parents have always been Republicans, but their Trump support really surprised me."

Her girls, she says, don't yet fully grasp what it means that Trump has carte blanche now that the House and Senate are also Republican, though her older one is worried about her little cousins, who emigrated from Turkey. She thinks they're aware of her own anxiety, but she doesn't believe in hiding her politics from them. "We have very frank talks where I've explained fascism and Marxism to them," she says. "I am very opinionated and I always answer their questions as they come—that open dialogue is essential. So is my never asking them to care about or pledge allegiance to things they don't care about. But they were not ambivalent about Trump, even though both sets of grandparents are supporters—I did not feel I had to influence them because they have a natural zero-tolerance policy toward bigotry."

"You have to teach children bigotry," Sara goes on. "My younger daughter was most upset about what Trump had to say about Mexicans, and especially the idea that people can be deported en masse or that a wall could be built to keep people out who wanted to improve lives for their children. She immediately started talking about how nobody would stand for that and how everyone would protest, while my older daughter thought he came across as crazy and unsafe to have as a president. So while sometimes I think they think I'm overly dramatic, ultimately I have confidence in my girls' views and in their father's and my ability to make them feel safe."

Making daughters feel safe in a Trump world, though, isn't easy. Jen Deaderick and her twelve-year-old daughter were canvassing for Hillary Clinton in New Hampshire last weekend when a man yelled "I'll grab your pussies!" at Jen's daughter and their friend as they held up Hillary signs. "She knows it's connected to Trump," says Deaderick, who lives outside of Boston.

"I had to convince her to go to school on Wednesday, so I compared it to when I went through September 11. It was scary to go into Manhattan, ride the subway, go into tall buildings. But we did it because we felt like if we didn't, then the terrorists win. That's when I realized this election feels like terrorism to me. But I reminded her of all the kids in her school who would be scared today, and told her it would be good for them to all be together, to take care of each other." Quelling her disappointment, however, is another matter entirely. "She said, 'You told me I was witnessing a vote for our first woman president!'"

Robin Marty's eight-and-a-half-year-old daughter, Violet, woke up on Wednesday and said, "You never woke me up," expecting to be roused to hear great news. "I had to tell her that Trump had won. Her face flushed and tears filled her eyes. I told her that sometimes the good guy doesn't win. It just means we have to try harder, and help the rest of our community along the way. That seemed to help."

When her daughter, who is the eldest of Marty's three kids, happened to catch the final ten minutes of the second debate, Trump became more real for her. "She was horrified—they were talking about the sexual-assault allegations. While we talk about how Republicans often don't support same-sex marriage or pay equity or why it's important to allow people from other countries to come here to be safe, this election felt too NC-17 to let her dig into. The idea that I had to shelter my child from a presidential campaign was horrifying. How do I tell her not to swear like the fifth-graders when she's watching a presidential candidate say 'bitch' or 'pussy'?"

But just as it is important to keep talking with our kids, it is also important to keep them, and ourselves, from feeling powerless. "I told Nic that it's young people like him who are the future, and that they will lead us out of this mess," said Villarosa. "But then I came correct: It's not just on his generation; all of us have to figure out together how to hold tight to our values and make our way back to what is real and right."

"I Love You, But . . .": What Your Trump Vote Tells My Family

David Valdes Greenwood

David Valdes Greenwood is an award-winning playwright, author, and journalist whose writing has appeared in the Boston Globe, AOL, *and elsewhere. He lives outside Boston.*

As the election approaches, I have not unfriended anyone on Facebook or turned away from them over their intended vote.

But I have to admit, when I hear people who love me say that they are voting for Donald Trump, it wounds.

I don't mean that I'm irked or politically offended; I mean that it hurts my heart to understand that someone who claims to care about my family can excuse or embrace a man who has denigrated just about every aspect of who we are.

When friends tell me Trump's "agenda" or "values" aligns better with their own, it chips away at my trust in how truly they care not just about people *like* me and my daughter but about us in specific.

It can't help but tarnish my affection, dimming the luster of a bond premised on the belief of mutual respect. Why? Because a vote for this man is a vote for what he says about us.

I know you're already thinking that this is unfair. That someone can still love us and vote differently. And that's true in most years. But this election has lowered the bar of discourse so far, has diminished the American embrace of human decency so thoroughly, that I don't really think that "I love you, but . . ." means very much when it comes to being loving right now. Hear me out.

I am a Latino son of an immigrant, and a gay dad to a daughter of African-American descent. To unpack how much Trump has said about facets of our lives is to stroll through a daily litany of mockery and dismissal. And when I look at what he has promised to do once elected, I see that we are a target.

When I adopted my daughter, everything was easier because my husband and I were legally married, something only true in two states at the time. At airports, hospitals, and schools, our legal bond to our child has never been in doubt.

Marriage equality has been one of the hallmarks of this century so far, now embraced by the majority of Americans, but Trump has said he's seriously considering what can be done to roll that right backward. He's also pledged to support legislation that would grant any person of any claimed faith the right not to serve or do business with any gay person. The bill is hatefully broad in its wording: we're not just talking the famed bakers of wedding cakes but landlords, health care providers, employers, and anyone with a business.

Like people who say they care for me, Trump says his gay friends are "fabulous" but that this is bigger than them. He doesn't think people like me need marriage rights for our families or the ability to shop, sleep, eat, and be cared for everywhere that our straight fellow citizens can.

That can only be because we are seen as lesser humans—which is, in fact, how he seems to see every group to which he doesn't belong. In my household, we represent a lot of those groups.

Take my daughter, a child of African-American descent. Trump calls all people like her "the Blacks"—a simple phrase that tells you so much. He has no sense of the diversity of the experience, whether in geography or values or status or needs. He has made this lack of perspective clear, by telling "the Blacks" that "their" schools, jobs, and lives are all terrible.

To Trump, people of color are so foreign—and so the antithesis of what he's selling—that he threw one of his own African-American supporters out of a rally last week, because he assumed the man to be an enemy on sight. (In fact, the man had previously praised Trump on the record.)

That's not surprising: When you decide an entire group of people is "the other," snap judgments are like breathing.

At least he considers "the Blacks" part of the nation. The last year and a half have been a time when Latinos—all 55 million of us in this country—have seen clearly what he really thinks of us.

It started with immigrants, all killers and rapists, to use his terms. (This applied only to *Latino* immigrants and not to people like his wife.) His venom expanded outward from there. When he said an Indiana-born judge couldn't be trusted because he was of Latino descent, and when he threw an award-winning reporter out of a press conference because of his Latino bias, Trump revealed his innate bent toward racist generalization.

His level of ignorance reached its peak when he said he actually loves "Hispanics," which he proved with a taco bowl. It was so base, so ridiculous, and so Trump. Reducing millions of diverse Americans to a food product for sale is just another reminder: To him, we aren't people.

And yet, *nothing* compares to the depths of Trump's grossness and crassness on the subject of women. This man wields women's looks as a cudgel, diminishing their worth and credibility based on his scale of beauty; he boasts about how conquests bolster a man's success; and he uses the topic of menstruation as a weapon.

He actively reveals a complete lack of boundaries when it comes to analyzing the bodies of women not just young enough to be his daughter, but his actual daughter, and girls far, far younger. It's been upsetting enough to take that all in as a human being, period. But as a parent, it's even worse.

It terrifies me. To vote for this man is to vote for the creepy uncle, the pervy boss, the guy who won't take no for an answer. His gleeful boasts about sexual misconduct were labeled "locker room talk" but now that locker room could be the White House.

To excuse it—over and over—is to tell him he's right in thinking that women and girls are less than men. To vote for someone so unapologetic in his sexism, to make him the face of your nation, is to tell girls that they must take whatever a man dishes out. No—it tells *everyone* this. And my daughter's future will be more dangerous as a result.

And these are just the messages of his words and deeds as they relate to my small household. I could expand outward to Muslim friends, my veteran relatives, or Jewish in-laws to reveal all the language and imagery Trump's campaign has deployed to make clear that they are "less than" him—and if they don't like it, there's more to come.

The imagery of this campaign is like none I can remember; when the KKK is doing "get out the vote" work for a candidate, it is no surprise that Trump signs show up effortlessly paired with lynched dummies or a bumper sticker depicting gay bashing. Trump didn't *make* these companion pieces himself, of course; but he has surely granted permission for people to not just indulge their worst thoughts, but to absolutely revel in them. He stoked a fire in people who have grown tired of making the effort to extend civility and human decency to those not like them.

What was once a goading whisper has become the roar of the crowd: *It's OK to embrace your secret feeling that all the "others" are not your people, are not equal to you, and, in being worth less, need not be treated with the same respect and privileges you enjoy.* Trump has made it fine not only to embrace this deeply un-American sentiment but to say it with pride, to shout it out loud alongside thousands of your exuberant peers.

And then to vote it.

If you love me and you're going to vote for Trump, I would like you to look me in the eye and say, "I'm OK with what Trump plans for you." If you love my daughter, whose growth you have followed with joy, I want you to look her in the eye and say, "I'm OK with how Trump talks about you."

Maybe dig out our holiday card from last year and, while looking at our smiling faces, practice saying to us: "You are less than me."

Because *that* is what your vote for Trump says to my family.

The Day After the Election, I Told My Daughter the Truth

Nicole Chung

Nicole Chung is a writer and editor based in Maryland.

IT WASN'T THE TALK I WANTED OR EXPECTED TO HAVE WITH MY eight-year-old, who beamed with such delight the day Hillary Clinton secured the Democratic nomination; who wanted to send money from her own piggy bank to Hillary's campaign; who begged me to buy her Hillary T-shirts (*Run Like a Girl*, *A Woman's Place Is in the White House*); who tagged along with me when I voted on Tuesday, saying, for the hundredth time, that she wished she could vote. Her faith in her candidate's victory was rock-solid, and it never occurred to me that it might be misplaced.

Tuesday night, when she pleaded with us to stay up late and watch election returns, I shrugged at my husband and said, "This is historic! Think of the memories she'll have." So we kept pushing her bedtime back, and back, until her questions and worried comments gradually slowed and she curled up next to me under a flowered quilt, electric-blue glasses askew, her carefully filled-out electoral map long discarded. When we finally sent her to her bed, I promised I'd wake her up and tell her if they called it for Hillary Clinton. "I hope it's soon," she said with a tired grin, as she padded down the hall to her room.

She still had hope, and so did I, but I was also afraid; my heart, which had been racing all night without pause, now felt faint. My husband and I would remain up for hours, alternately swearing and reaching for each other's hands in bleary and increasing panic. *This will turn around,* I kept thinking, *it has to, and when it does I'll go wake up our daughter and give her the good news.*

As my husband and I sent texts and emails, refreshed site after site, our daughter kept sleeping. She slept all through the night.

I can't pretend this election hasn't felt achingly, frighteningly personal. A vote for Trump was always going to be a vote *against* black Americans, Muslim Americans, immigrant Americans; against women and LGBTQ people and people with disabilities. Since Tuesday night, I have been grappling with the sadness and terror I feel as the parent of two girls who are not white, one of whom has a disability; as a woman, a child of immigrants, and a person in a multiracial, multicultural family. I have enormous privilege, and I am also one of millions of people who now feel less safe here.

"Whiteness always wins," one of my (white) friends said to me. She wasn't shocked; why, I wondered, was I? Why hadn't I seen this coming? While I'm never especially surprised by white supremacy or misogyny or bigotry—while I thought the election would be wrenchingly close, and always expected to feel depressed by the sheer number of my fellow citizens, including many people I know and love, who cast their votes for Trump—I never actually thought he could win.

My shock now seems further proof of my privilege, a misplaced faith I find utterly mystifying. The question unspooling in my mind as I watched the returns come in that night, the question I kept asking my husband and our equally horrified and bewildered friends, was how on earth we would face our children and clear the breakfast table gauntlet the morning after. How could we possibly explain to our daughter that, given the choice between a hardworking, imperfect, eminently qualified stateswoman and a reality-television star running on a platform of hatred and fear, so many people—including many of our neighbors, friends, some of our family members—chose the latter?

Rationally, I know that all of us have far more to fear than these wretched conversations we'll have, over and over for the next four years, with our children. But I can't help but feel as though I let both my kids down; that I lied to them when I said I was sure our country wouldn't elect a man who'd shown himself to be so utterly unqualified, who campaigned and won with grandstanding displays of vicious contempt for so many Americans. When I told them I thought he couldn't win, what I was really telling them was, *In spite of everything, I still believe this is your country, and I want you to believe it too.*

Though the outcome of the election was in little doubt by midnight, I stayed up until nearly four in the morning, reading the first postmortems alongside texts from friends and desperately trying to cobble together what to say to my older child, come daylight. What I kept coming back to, over and over, seemed too devastating to tell an innocent and hopeful eight-year-old: *I thought we were better than this. I was wrong.*

Our older daughter asked us as soon as she woke up. Trump won, we said, and Hillary lost. She looked crestfallen, and we resisted the urge to try and make it better, cheer her up. The worry and disappointment and anger you feel right now—all of those feelings are okay, we told her. This is terrible news, and nothing can make it better.

We pointed out that we—our family—will be all right for now. We are an interracial family; every once in a while, we might not feel 100% welcome in a given space. But we live in a blue state, and we have more than our share of advantages. If the worry isn't chiefly ours, we told our daughter, the responsibility is. We need to be ready to help others, defend their rights and stand with their families.

We tried to explain why this happened. A lot of men do not respect girls and women, whatever they might say. A lot of white people in this country are afraid of those who don't look like them, or believe all the things they believe. They feel left behind; they are looking for people to blame. They have a vision of how this country should be that is, was *always*, false. Our child nodded along as we told her this; she's heard it from us before. Yes, people are angry, we said, and some of them have cause. But it doesn't matter how justified your frustration is—you do not take what power you do have and use it to hurt others, or make them feel less safe.

Our daughter, who is a lot like me and therefore always wants to know The Plan, asked what she could do. Well, we said, you're already doing something. You can try to be an especially good friend. Be compassionate. Be angry when your friends are angry for a good reason. Be the kind of person someone might reach out to if they are sad, or scared, or lonely, or being bullied. Look out for everyone—especially the kids who seem a little out of place, who might not have many friends.

This election, we told her, proves that you can't listen only to the things people *say* about who they are and what they believe. You have to watch them and see what they do. Respect has to be earned; not everyone in possession of authority deserves it—and that includes our new president. The day after we elected Donald Trump, I told my daughter the truth: This was the wrong choice. I am devastated. I am furious. And I am sorry, because you deserve better.

* * *

When my daughter asked me yesterday if we would ever leave the country, I said I was still glad to be raising her and her sister here, as opposed to a place where everyone looks the same, talks the same, believes the same things. Maybe it's something I told her because I wanted to offer her some comfort. It's almost something I have to tell myself, because we have nowhere else to go. But this slim and slippery thread of hope seems real enough when I follow it to its source: Many people in our country believe that our differences do not have to make us strangers; that they do, in fact, make us stronger. I hope that one day—in my kids' lifetimes—those who know that will outnumber the people who don't.

I've been thinking a lot about the tension between anger and hope after this strangest, most stressful of election years, and how I'm glad my child has managed to absorb some of both. But on the dreadful day after, it was hard not to feel guilty as I dropped my kids off at school. Maybe it was a mistake telling my older daughter so much. Maybe I built up her hopes too high. Maybe, now that she has learned this latest terrible lesson about America, the hope she does have will wither before it can take root, flourish, and bear fruit.

But then, I know that I can only give her the truth, and what she does with it is her choice. She could never have remained unaware, in any case: We've never shied away from discussing the hard things with her, and kids are always aware of so much more than parents think. Our child came home with questions about why Trump didn't like immigrants weeks before he'd even clinched the nomination. She was annoyed that in the lead-up to her school's mock election, the teachers told them facts about Trump's family and business, but "nothing about the bad things he's said." She is thoughtful, and curious, with a stubborn and growing love of justice. This election year and its horrific aftermath would not have escaped her notice, no matter what her father and I chose to share with her.

None of us who parent or play a role in kids' lives can afford to flinch or look away from the ugliness of the election, because its consequences will play out in the lives and communities of those too young to vote. I believe they need to hear the truth from us—now more than ever. They must know what they are up against, so they can plan; see what their friends are up against, so they can stand with them. If this election's results have betrayed their trust, withholding the facts in the interest of "protecting" them would be another kind of failure.

My daughter and I talked some more about the election and her friends' shock and worry when she got home from school yesterday. The girls were all sad, she said, because "they really wanted a woman to be president." She added that one boy in particular seemed "a little worried." His family is Muslim, and he had been one of the kids she talked with most often about the presidential race, one who seemed aware and genuinely anxious about what would happen. "I didn't say anything to him about the election," my daughter said quickly, as if to reassure me before I could ask. "I just sat next to him at lunch, and asked how he was."

Today, she sat next to me in her messy, book-cluttered bedroom, wearing her *Run Like a Girl* shirt with the Hillary Clinton logo, watching her concession speech on my laptop. I wanted to show it to her because of what Hillary had said directly to her and others like her: "To all of the little girls who are watching this, never doubt that you are valuable and powerful and deserving of every chance and opportunity in the world to pursue and achieve your own dreams."

When it was over, my daughter looked at me and said, "I'm still sad, but I feel a little better. We'll try to stop Donald Trump from doing all the bad things he wants to do. And I think there will be a woman president someday." For all the worry and anger I've known since election night, all the moments when I've felt myself slide into despair, I still want to believe she's right.

Fliers on the Train

Carlos Sandoval

Carlos Sandoval is the producer/director of the award-winning films
Farmingville, A Class Apart *and* The State of Arizona. *He lives in*
Amagansett.

HATE HURTS MOST WHEN YOU'RE NOT READY FOR IT, WHEN YOUR
thoughts after a brutal political season are of the comfort of home.
That's how hate sliced through me recently on the Long Island Rail
Road—suddenly. I spotted it out of the corner of my eye. Two KKK
fliers, neatly placed face up, inviting passers-by to collect them. "Our
Race Is Our Nation" read the banner on one, with a white-hooded
figure peering out through slits where eyes should be, his arms folded
defiantly behind the safety of symbol and disguise.

The fliers had their intended effect. They hurled me back to that
place of self-preservation I constructed as a child. Fold yourself small,
don't call attention, smile, and you may get by. But you'll never get
in. You'll never fully be accepted as American. Despite your five-
generation presence and fancy degrees you're still asked pointedly or

with guarded emphasis, "Where are you from?" The guy in the hoodie is right: This is a nation defined by race.

As I stared at the flier, I thought of Lexi, my fifteen-year-old great-niece who lives in my hometown in Southern California. Lexi is a smart and curious kid. At age twelve she was an autodidact about World War II, inspired in part by having read the poignant novel "All the Light We Cannot See." She knows more about the rise of fascism and terrors of totalitarianism than I, or maybe it's all fresher to her because last year her reading list included *Fahrenheit 451*.

Lexi's mother, my niece, generally leans Christian conservative. Lexi found Bernie Sanders on her own. She was excited about him even before his unlikely candidacy began to take off. A pragmatist, she took to Hillary Clinton after the convention. While I monitored her political education from afar, I hadn't tracked her response to Donald Trump's insurgency, it was too remote a possibility to consider.

I shared the KKK flier with Lexi's mom, who in turn shared it with Lexi. When we spoke with Lexi, I realized her world had been shattered by the election. It is now occupied by terror based on half-accurate assumptions. I recognized in her inchoate trauma my own childhood reaction to the Cuban missile crisis, when headlines balled into nightmares from which I'd wake up too scared to scream.

Lexi is afraid she may be deported because her estranged Cuban-born father may never have taken care of the details of his otherwise legal immigration status and was temporarily detained after a run-in with the law. "I've heard some people want to make it so that I could get deported because I'm an anchor baby." No, I assure her, you are not an "anchor baby." You are a U.S. citizen by birth and through your mother. The Constitution still stands. Oh, the pain of living under political rumors and half-truths when you're young and your life is at stake.

"Okay," she replies softly from the phone, but I sense things remain unsettled. I probe. She answers, "I have friends whose parents are undocumented." She goes on, "I hear things like, 'If it ain't white it ain't right.'"

I look at the KKK flier. I find myself unable to give Lexi much comfort or guidance. I realize we have lost or, at the very least, stunted another generation. Maybe the flier is partly right: Race is our nation.

To steady myself, I try being rational. We live in a world in which fear has been frothed way beyond the rational facts. Wages are up, unemployment down, so domestic economic indicators are solid. The crime rate is generally down. Health care coverage has expanded, albeit imperfectly. Peace exists throughout the Western Hemisphere, indeed throughout the world, with the glaring exception of the raw swaths that cut through the Middle East and eastern Africa. These are among America's greatest days, our days of greatest potential, but apparently a lot of us don't see it that way.

To understand why, I reach beyond reason to my emotions, back to my childhood, to get at the despair created by gutted-out industrial sectors in the Midwest, the sense of abandonment in coal territory, the anxiety of family farmers we once held as our American ideal but who now can't hold on to the farm without an outside job.

My own roots are deep in the working class. My father was a union man who washed the soiled diapers of patients at a large mental institution. My mother was a garment worker at a tiny factory that produced itchy gym clothes. Each put in hours after their regular workday to earn enough to make ends meet. Mama stayed on to clean the garment factory; Dad mowed lawns. I know how hard they worked because it was my job to sometimes help them after school. I know how much they worried because I caught my mother behind closed doors, her head hanging while tears formed quietly because there wasn't enough to carry us through the week. I knew we'd be okay when she got up the next morning at 4:30 to start over again.

I can feel the ache of white opioid-addicted youth in Maine, rural

Ohio, or eastern Kentucky. Despair litters their land, just as it did the land of my childhood, in a small, loving, but ultimately dangerous suburban barrio saddled with drugs and gang activity. One of my close family members ran with the gangs and was left overdosed in our front yard.

Despair comes from disaffection, a fact we in communities of color have known for generations. With the devil of addiction now knocking at its own door, white America is finally realizing that we communities of color weren't sociopathological after all, we were just human, humans from whom hope and opportunity had been systematically withheld, just as our impoverished white brothers and sisters are discovering has happened to them.

From my now-privileged position I am coming to realize that the fear I saw in the KKK fliers wasn't just mine, but also that of the people who put the fliers on the seats. It's a recurrent fear in America. The Klan has come and gone in cycles. The first was during Reconstruction. The second in the 1920s, when the Klan populated Long Island because of an anti-immigrant backlash—ironically enough aimed at the parents and grandparents of many people the Klan hopes to recruit now, citing the newer wave of immigrants. The third Klan wave was during the civil rights struggle of the 1960s. All times of change.

In filming *The State of Arizona*, our documentary about Arizona's controversial "show me your papers" law, we interviewed a very wise young state legislator. She pointed out that the people who had crossed the U.S.-Mexico border illegally had had time to make the emotional journey into change. The communities receiving them hadn't, however, and so the intensity of their anger could in part be understood by the rapid, unexpected change foisted on them. Her contextualization helped me reframe my perspective then, and I find it useful now as I try to understand the KKK fliers and the sundering of America they are trying to foment.

So, the next time I speak with Lexi, I'll explain that we, all of us, need to understand that the challenges America is facing aren't just its transforming features; after all, people of color are also being impacted by the forces of technology and globalization, even more so. I'll tell her that despite the pain it will take to get past the scapegoating, I hope that I and others like me who have been marginalized and fought for change can reach out and show how change can be accomplished; we've done it.

I'll go on to tell her that the person who left the fliers most likely descends from a brave immigrant who chose change, willingly suffering hardships and upsetting the landscape before them, forging America in the process. Maybe someday they'll realize that.

In a Time of Trump, Millennial Jews Awaken to Anti-Semitism

Benjamin Wofford

Benjamin Wofford is a contributing editor at POLITICO *Magazine.*

LIKE MANY JEWISH FAMILIES IN AMERICA, THE REIZES HOUSEHOLD has been deliberating in recent months what Donald Trump *really* thinks of them.

As they celebrate the Jewish New Year this weekend in their suburban Cleveland home, the topic of discussion will once again be anti-Semitism, and whether it's surging in the United States thanks to the Trump campaign. Like others representing America's aging Jewish Gen-X'ers and boomers, Joelle Reizes, forty-eight, remembers experiencing some anti-Semitism as a girl—occasional sideways glances and untoward comments. But millennial Jews and their juniors are another matter. Joelle's children—ages nineteen, fourteen, and twelve—have grown up during an unprecedented era of prosperity and assimilation for Jews in America, one in which the struggles endured by an earlier generation are understood as something closer to historical lore than present fact.

"They've been protected," says the Reizes' mother, "to help them to feel like being Jewish isn't different."

For younger Jews in the United States, that era has suddenly passed. The early months of 2016 brought in a strange tide of online hate speech aimed largely at Jewish journalists who had published articles critical of Trump or his campaign, with all the old ugly epithets on display. Then in July Trump's Twitter account posted an image of a six-pointed star next to a picture of Hillary Clinton, with a pile of money in the background. Though he deleted the tweet, afterward Trump walked up to a brightly lit podium and defended the image, bellowing that the Jewish star was not a Jewish star. A dim reality descended on American Jews. Yes: Trump had broadcast the message of a neo-Nazi without apology.

The issue roared back into view in September, when the ex-wife of Trump's campaign CEO, Steve Bannon, said that Bannon had kept his daughters out of a school because there were too many "whiny" Jewish brats there; the candidate's son, Donald Trump, Jr., retweeted someone described as the neo-Nazis' "favorite academic"; and a Trump advisor was accused of discriminating against Jewish employees (and denying the Holocaust).* Then Don Trump, Jr., with unblinking casualness, stumbled on an odious analogy. "The media has been [Clinton's] number one surrogate," Donald, Jr. complained, not unlike a whiny brat, during a radio interview in Philadelphia. "If Republicans were doing that, they'd be warming up the gas chamber."

---

* Nancy Dillon, "Anti-Semitic Trump Campaign CEO Stephen Bannon Not a Big Fan of 'Whiny Brat' Jews, Ex-Wife Says," *New York Daily News*, August 27, 2016, www .nydailynews.com/news/election/trump-campaign-ceo-bannon-complained-jews -daughters-school-article-1.2767615; Ari Feldman, "Donald Trump Jr. Retweets the 'Neo-Nazi Movement's Favorite Academic,'" *Forward*, September 1, 2016, forward. com/news/national/348960/donald-trump-jr-retweets-the-neo-nazi-movements -favorite-academic/; Eugene Daniels, "Trump Adviser Accused of Anti-Semitism," *AJC*, August 19, 2016.

Trump himself, of course, has denied any hint of anti-Semitism, pointing out that his daughter Ivanka is married to an Orthodox Jew, Jared Kushner, who is also a close campaign advisor. Even so, the Reizes family of Cleveland has been deliberating how to process such events—and the return of an age-old enmity that the Trump campaign has somehow reawakened. How soon is too soon to brush the cobwebs away from an ancient alarm bell? The father, Ofer Reizes, a soft-spoken man of Israeli heritage, wants to discern the source before issuing labels. "My reservation with how anti-Semitic Mr. Trump really is is that he's playing a game, a very effective game," he says. His wife prods back: "I don't *care* if he's playing a game or not." "It's just part of his campaign, is my point," Mr. Reizes retorts in plaintive, be-understanding tone. "It's the *people* he's riling up." There's a pause, as his wife quietly considers this. "When David Duke thinks he's the best thing ever," she intones slowly, "it doesn't matter what [Trump] feels in his heart."

But while his parents deliberate, it's nineteen-year-old Zach Reizes who is most firm in his views. "What Trump has brought to the surface is, in many ways, the first blatant anti-Semitic experience for the vast majority of American millennials," says Zach, an angular and handsome sophomore at Ohio University. On campus, he's active both with AIPAC, the right-of-center bulwark of Jewish politics, and J-Street, its younger and left-leaning rival. "My little sister," he adds, thinks that Trump "is the [evil king's advisor] Haman of the Purim story."

Trump's success—and a white nationalist subculture blooming like algae in the Internet's unlighted depths—has turned millennial Jews into the new expositors of anti-Semitism at the dinner table: quietly explaining Pepe the Frog, opaque Twitter memes and dyspeptic forums like Stormfront to frozen audiences of parents and grandparents. It's thrust young Jews into long-buried questions of assimilation and political position, whiteness and privilege. And it's heightened a divide between young and old, left and right: Progressive young Jews learning to form the words "anti-Semitism," often for the first time—even while they take umbrage at their right-leaning scolds who, now into October, have kept up a deafening silence on the topic of Trump.

This year, Reizes and his peers have watched the situation deteriorate: headshots of journalists superimposed in concentration camps; calls to Jewish reporters in the middle of the night playing Hitler's voice; white supremacists who appended parentheses around the names of Jews online. Recently, a feature by *POLITICO* on white America won its author fresh opprobrium as a "Marxist kike." The anonymous stalker's Twitter avatar, Pepe the Frog, has become a symbol of the white nationalist alt-right—named by the Anti-Defamation League as an official hate symbol—and an image that Donald Trump himself once broadcast, amplifying the dog whistles of a more innocent era into something akin to a trombone blast.

To some young Jews, this election season has felt like a cold shower. "Whether you experienced no anti-Semitism growing up, or a watered-down version of it, I think most young people felt like anti-Semitism was dying," says Debbie Rabbinovich, nineteen, a sophomore and Hillel member at the University of Pennsylvania. Other young activists were reconsidering what they had heard for years from an older generation. "For a long time we were told that anti-Semitism was everywhere, and we rolled our eyes at that," says Morriah Kaplan, twenty-four, a leader in the left-leaning activist group If Not Now. But, she acknowledged, "This feels like the closest thing to the type of anti-Semitism that my grandparents talk about experiencing in Poland."

When I spoke with Zach Reizes not long ago, his fears had amplified—as well as a sense among young Jews that America's right-leaning Jewish elite was losing credibility. "Most college students are handling this type of anti-Semitism for the first time," Reizes said. There's a sense that "it delegitimizes the position of far right wing activists [in Jewish politics] who support a candidate who is, at least in some ways, tacitly anti-Semitic."

It's impossible, as American Jewish families go, to gauge how widespread these dinner table conversations are—but the scope and scale was hinted at when the discord touched the family of Haman himself. When Donald Trump's star tweet sufficiently embarrassed Jared Kushner, Trump's Orthodox son-in-law, Kushner published an op-ed in his paper, the *New York Observer*, defending Trump and invoking the plight of his ancestors in the Holocaust. Immediately, Kushner's extended family fired back, launching an internecine war of words: "Please don't invoke our grandparents in vain just so you can sleep better at night," seethed one Kushner cousin. "It is self-serving and disgusting."

Kushner was also blasted by a young member of his staff at the *New York Observer*, twenty-three-year-old writer Dana Schwartz, who is Jewish. Her provocation was an open letter, and it was scathing. "When you stand silent and smiling in the background, his Jewish son-in-law," she wrote to her boss, "you're giving his most hateful supporters tacit approval."

"Donald Trump," Reizes says, "has put the Jewish community in a turmoil that I don't really think we've experienced in a long time."

Presidential politics has never been entirely immune from this disease. In 1935, FDR spoke of "dirty Jewish tricks" to describe a tax maneuver by the *New York Times*, and ribbed a sitting senator about the lack of "Jewish blood in our veins." Harry Truman's diary revealed not dissimilar sentiments. Rumors of Richard Nixon's tirades chased his campaigns long before becoming president. After he won in 1968, White House tapes reveal a president speaking freely of Jewish cabals controlling the media and the IRS. He also included fairly straightforward instructions about his judicial nominees: "No Jews. Is that clear?" (It was.) Nixon's became the last tenure of semi-public, anti-Semitic overtures—a political milestone that also demarked a moment of assimilation for American Jewry.

But in this moment, the silence on anti-Semitism—at a juncture of world-historical importance, on an international stage—is a problem that afflicts only one side, not two. Millennial Jews have noticed. If students don't hear from the Jewish right on Trump, and soon, says Marjorie Feld, a professor whose research focus is on Jewish American history, "there may be a price to pay in terms of [the Jewish Right's] own longevity."

Young American Jews have identified a problem. But it's with trepidation. As the establishment clashes, millennial Jews may still be deliberating if, and how, to take sides. It's a delicate balancing act. To be a center-left Jew in American politics is often to internalize two suspicions simultaneously: insufficiently moved by the plight of the marginalized on campus; and insufficiently moved for the plight of Israel at the family reunion.

"What I always heard from my grandparents and my mom were very stereotypical examples of anti-Semitism," says Reizes. "I always said, this is dying out. Maybe in Europe." The election has caused enough students to ask aloud—were the grandparents right? "It's a moment when both you and your grandma get to be right about this," Harpo Jaeger, twenty-five, an experienced campus activist in Jewish politics and a faith-based organizer, tells me. "She gets to be right that anti-Semitism is alive and well, and Jews should be worried about it," he adds. "And the left gets to be correct, in that the anti-Israel or anti-Zionist left doesn't have a monopoly on anti-Semitism. These people really are everywhere."

Then there is the dilemma on campus. Even as they might march with Black Lives Matter or once lobbied for marriage equality, on campus, says Rabbinovich, "Anti-Semitism isn't viewed as an important or valid form of prejudice." Partly for this reason, Reizes suspects more Jewish students are leery of bringing up anti-Semitism, whether in class, on Twitter or in person. "Many of us don't know how to tackle it," says Reizes. "The inability to . . . to fight back against it comes from a few places," he adds. "But I also think it comes from a hesitancy to maybe support Judaism because of Israel."

It would be a mistake to blame Boycott, Divest, Sanctions (BDS), a movement that seeks to put economic and political pressure on Israel and that has been supported by many millennials, for this condition. More likely, efforts like the "Jew Haters" campaign—in which UCLA student David Horowitz papered campus with posters that read "Jew Hater" under the headshots of UCLA undergraduates—have done much to raise the political price of speaking out. "A lot of young Jews don't have the vocabulary to talk about anti-Semitism, because most of the time the label is levelled against us and those we would align with—like those who called for acknowledging human rights of Palestinians," says Kaplan. "That's language we've separated ourselves from." One Brown University senior told me "there's no question" that Trump is peddling anti-Semitism. But there won't be a "Jews Against Trump" rally at Brown any time soon. The charge of anti-Semitism, the senior said, would just "get caught in their throat, because there's so much psychological baggage about grandma, and psychological baggage about being gas-lighted" by the far right.

The Jewish right has long pushed the message that we can't talk of Israel without talking of anti-Semitism. Not without irony, then, have they gotten their wish: a generation of left-leaning Jews ready to speak publically against anti-Semitism, yet frozen by fear that it appears disingenuous to do so, convinced it's viewed as code for Israel. Trump's rhetoric may be unprecedented. But no one wants to join an inquisition that marks their hall mates as Jew Haters.

The dilemma on campus offers a metaphor for the 2016 campaign, one that has enlarged a dilemma occupying the minds of American Jews, not just young ones. Empowered majority or embattled minority? Ally or victim? At the heart of this tumult is a sensitive question, one millennials haven't had much reason to engage until now: How white are the Jews?

This divide between two Judaisms—splitscreen worlds of historical memory, privilege and whiteness—may never be bridged. If it can, millennials may be the ones who bridge it. In July, Jewish activist Carly Pildis penned an essay in *Tablet* magazine, "I am Woke," urging activists of the left to accept the reality of anti-Semitism into their sensibility of social justice, without Jews apologizing for Israel. "We are facing a wave of anger and violence against people of color not seen in my lifetime," writes Pildis. "The Jewish people are facing that, too, the anger, the violent rhetoric, the Trump supporters demanding Jewish reporters' heads."

That message resonates with Rabbinovich, the Penn sophomore, who wants to see anti-Semitism reconsidered as the kind of structural oppression taught on campuses. "I think for that to happen, young people on the center-left have to be calling it out," she says. "I think it's kind of a brave step for people on the center-left to take, because it's so unfamiliar. But it's also the right step." But she also sees Trump as a moral imperative for Jews to find common cause with the social justice activism of the moment, not just that of Israel.

These conversations—difficult, tangled—may soon bear out, when the Reizes and other families convene over the High Holy Days, beginning with Rosh Hashanah. Millennials are in a good position to lead these conversations; explainers of a strange new world, much of it online, and ambassadors of a campus generation more attuned to the politics of social justice than in recent memory. But each generation will have much to share.

"Why the Jews? I don't know," says Zach Reizes. "It's a very scary thought, that maybe all those horror stories we've been told about Jewish persecution are right." The nineteen-year-old adds, "Maybe they're still foreshadowing a future that we thought had died."

"I haven't gotten to sit down for a real talk with my parents," Dana Schwartz, the author of the open letter that pricked Kushner to action, told me over the summer. "I'm actually going home to Chicago this weekend. That's where the conversation will happen."

"I Had a Scary Dream About Donald Trump": Muslim Parents Face a Tense Election

Samantha Schmidt

Samantha Schmidt is a Morning Mix *reporter at the* Washington Post. *She lives in Washington, D.C.*

BILAL ELCHARFA WAS POURING CEREAL FOR HIS CHILDREN BEFORE school this month when his seven-year-old daughter, Maaria, walked into the kitchen, calling for him.

"Baba, I had a scary dream," she said, hugging him tight. "About Donald Trump."

It was the morning after the second presidential debate, which the Elcharfa family's two youngest daughters watched in the basement of their Staten Island home with their parents. In the middle of the night, Maaria went to her parents' room twice, unable to sleep, and walked to the living room and checked her family's security camera.

That morning, Mr. Elcharfa, fifty-two, asked his daughter what she saw in the nightmare.

"He was so mean to us," she said. "He had a scary face, like a zombie or something." In the dream, Maaria later said, Mr. Trump came to the home of every Muslim family in the country and put each one in jail.

"Don't worry," he told his daughter, comforting her. "He's just talk."

He tried to sound convincing. But her nightmare unsettled him. Mr. Elcharfa and his wife had fled war in their native Lebanon in the hopes of raising a family in safety in the United States. Mr. Elcharfa, a taxi driver, had dealt with his own share of anti-Muslim sentiment, like the time a passenger refused to pay his fare because he said Muslims needed to pay for the Sept. 11, 2001, attacks.

But for innocent Maaria, who still loves playing dress-up and pretending she is a princess, to experience it? Never had he felt so helpless.

"I'm trying to let my kids live in peace," he said. "I don't want them to worry."

Maaria is just beginning to understand that her family's faith sets her apart in her public school, where she is one of only a few Muslims in her second-grade class. But she does not fully grasp how it could be used against her, and she lacks the ability of even her older siblings, in their teens, to absorb the blows.

"They cannot defend themselves," Mr. Elcharfa said about Maaria and her nine-year-old sister, Zaynub. "They're still young."

Across the country, Muslim parents have been facing such moments almost daily, riding each tumultuous wave of the news cycle, including Mr. Trump's incendiary rhetoric and calls to ban Muslims from entering the country and the recent bombing in Manhattan. But how to explain such harsh realities to a young child?

Even as some Muslim parents try to shelter their children from the news, they cannot prevent them from hearing hurtful words in their classrooms and at the playground. Their children come home asking their parents why a classmate said Mr. Trump, the Republican nominee, wants to kick their family out of the country. They ask why, if their religion is one of peace, they so often get called terrorists in the hallways.

Many Muslim parents fear that the tensions could push their children away from the faith entirely. They are struggling with how to balance guiding their children in practicing and defending their religion, and letting them embrace it—or not—on their own terms.

"We don't know how to handle it sometimes," Mr. Elcharfa said. "Maybe someday they won't believe in anything."

The pressures are intense on Staten Island, a Republican stronghold and New York City's whitest borough. A few blocks from the Elcharfa home in the South Beach neighborhood, a large flag for Mr. Trump's campaign flaps in the wind, and a Trump sign is prominent in a yard around the corner.

Many of the family's Muslim friends have pulled their children out of public school and put them in private Islamic schools.

One of them, Somaia Saie, made that decision more than a year ago for her youngest children, ages nine and eleven, because she felt it was the "only way to keep the kids in a safe environment."

"I have no clue how we can raise children like this," Ms. Saie said. "As grown-ups, we can take it. With children, it's another story."

Last spring, the Elcharfas' nine-year-old, Zaynub, was sitting on the carpet in her third-grade classroom when two boys said to her, "If Donald Trump becomes president, he's going to kick you out of the country."

That night, frightened, she asked her mother about it. "Are we going to get kicked out? Where are we going to go?"

Her mother, Nayla Elhamoui, assured her that no president could do that. "That will never affect us," she told her daughter. "We belong here." She called the school's parent coordinator the next day. The principal met with the students and instructed them to apologize to Zaynub.

Mr. Elcharfa first came to the United States in the mid-1980s, and Ms. Elhamoui joined him about a decade later, after marrying him in

Lebanon. Their five children, ages seven to eighteen, were all born in the United States.

Ms. Elhamoui tells them the story of a terrifying night in Beirut when a bomb exploded across the street from her house. She was about eight years old. The shrapnel hit her leg, leaving her with scars. It took years before she could sleep without holding somebody's hand.

"See, be thankful we brought you up here," she said to her children on a recent afternoon, as she served them a Lebanese wheat dish called freekeh at their dining room table.

The Elcharfas' home is dotted with references to Arab and Muslim culture. Their couches are gold-trimmed. A kitchen clock marks the Islamic call to prayer. Their children speak fluent Arabic and have taken Quran classes.

But they also could not be more stereotypically American. The four youngest children all attend public school. Abubeckr, thirteen, loves video games and dreams of playing in the N.B.A. Maaria puts on make-up in her pink-walled bedroom, and Zaynub, a gymnast, does flips in the kitchen, wearing a pink shirt that says, "Leave sparkles wherever you go."

Mr. Elcharfa often tells his children they are American first, before they are Lebanese.

"We tell them this is your country," he said. "You're lucky you're born here."

But sometimes, in school, classmates only see the children's Muslim names and Arab heritage. In the hallways in Abubeckr's school, boys will sometimes make sounds of bombs exploding and yell out "Allahuakbar"—Arabic for "God is great"—as he walks by. On the bus after school, a classmate once said to him, "You're a terrorist, and your mom is a mastermind bomber."

He told the principal the next day, but he did not tell his parents. He is used to the jeering at this point, Abubeckr said, and does not want his mother to "make it a bigger deal than it is." His father has taught him to tell an adult, but not to react physically or verbally. "If you ignore it, it's better," Abubeckr said.

But Mr. Elcharfa sees the taunts taking a toll on his children. They frequently ask him not to speak in Arabic in front of their friends. After the recent explosion in the Chelsea neighborhood of Manhattan, his fifteen-year-old, Ismail, told him, "That's your Islam, Baba."

Abubeckr, who was in Italian class when he heard the news, thought to himself, It was a Muslim, wasn't it? "I was like, here we go again," he said, recounting that day while sitting with his father in the family's living room.

"Why do you say a Muslim; why don't you say a person?" Mr. Elcharfa asked his son.

These are the moments that worry Mr. Elcharfa and his wife. They fret that their children are starting to distance themselves from their religion and their culture. These are also the moments when the couple's parenting styles clash.

Mr. Elcharfa wants his children to be freethinkers. He does not want them to be practicing Muslims simply because they inherited the religion from their parents. Sometimes, he said, he wishes their religion could be hidden from view. He said he felt pangs of regret for giving them Muslim names: "Why didn't I name them Tony or George?"

His wife scoffs at such comments.

"I'm totally different," Ms. Elhamoui said. "We have to guide them. I have to push him and the kids to pray, to go to the mosque."

Their contrasting approaches played out in their kitchen this month, in a conversation over whether Zaynub should begin wearing a hijab. Ms. Elhamoui encourages both Zaynub and Maaria to wear a head scarf to school a couple of times a year, as "practice," she said. She bribes them, offering ice cream or chocolate.

"Zaynub says, 'I don't want to wear hijab; it's embarrassing,'"

Mr. Elcharfa told his wife, while he chopped peppers and cooked beans over the stove. He did not want his daughter to face the taunts that often come. "Let her choose," he said. "It's O.K. as long as she dresses nice and conservatively. It's not the way you look. It's the way you believe."

Ms. Elhamoui insisted they should encourage their daughter to try it. "It's in the religion," she said.

Similarly, when Maaria turned seven a few weeks ago, she began to pray multiple times a day with her parents, in exchange for a $10 allowance at the end of the week, which she keeps in a blue bear-shaped bank. Mr. Elcharfa acknowledges the importance of prayer, but does not agree with his wife's incentives.

"It's not easy, believe me," he said about these parenting disagreements. "That's why we keep fighting."

One decision was easy for the parents to make: During the third presidential debate on Wednesday, and other future speeches by Mr. Trump, the children would not be watching it.

"I don't want her to be scared," Ms. Elhamoui said, thinking again of Maaria's nightmare.

Maaria said that if Mr. Trump became president, "I'm going to stay in my room forever."

Mr. Elcharfa expressed frustration at what his family's life had become. He thought he had left behind conflicts over religion in Lebanon, where sectarian tensions cast a long shadow.

"I came here and found the same things following me," he said.

Sitting in the family's living room one recent morning, Ms. Elhamoui asked one of her daughters why she liked being a Muslim. The nine-year-old said she felt proud thinking about the Prophet Muhammad and the way he led his friends and followers in spreading peace.

Ms. Elhamoui reminded her daughter about the time the boys in her class made the comment about Mr. Trump's threat to kick Muslims out of the country. She asked, "What did you do to follow the Prophet Muhammad?"

Zaynub said she forgave the boys. Her mother smiled, nodding.

"We forgive," her mother reiterated. "So we can always live in peace."

Should I Teach My Kids to Value Truth in the Era of Trump?

John Ziegler

John Ziegler is a columnist, talk show host, and documentary filmmaker based in Los Angeles.

I AM THE FATHER OF AN ADORABLE/FEISTY FOUR-YEAR-OLD DAUGHTER named Grace, and my wife is pregnant with another girl due in the spring. Like most parents, I have thought long and hard about what kind of principles I should try to teach them to prepare them for life. I was brought up believing, mostly because my mother drilled it into my DNA, that truth was the ultimate value. I thought that if you told the truth, while things wouldn't always go right, in the end, everything would turn out okay. In short, I tried to live by the old credo that honesty was the best policy.

However, throughout my professional and personal life I learned that this premise is usually false, and sometimes catastrophically so. Still, like a gambler throwing good money after bad, I have continued to live based on this principle long after I had concluded that it was, at best, ineffective and, at times, simply soul-crushing.

What I haven't been able to figure out is whether my mother gave me really bad advice for how to live, or if the rules of the game have just dramatically changed since the 1970s when my understanding of society began to form. As with most confounding questions, the answer probably consists of a bit of both of these explanations, and probably a bit more.

Recently, I had two situations emerge with my daughter that took this issue out of the theoretical and put it into the practical for me. Both were rather cute, but also raised serious questions about how I would actually deal with real-life circumstances now that she is starting to be able to understand the world around her in significant ways.

The first occurred when I was heading from our home in California to Pennsylvania for a court hearing related to the "Penn State Scandal" which I have been investigating for years. Grace knows that Pennsylvania is where the "bad guys" in my crusade for justice live, and just before I left she earnestly handed me a "magic" rock complete with special words to say in order to fight the "bad guys" off.

When I returned from the trip, the subject of the "magic" rock came up and I played along, asking her what the talisman was supposed to do (because it hadn't worked at all). Much to my shock she immediately gave up the story entirely, saying, almost mockingly, "Dad, the stone isn't really magic. That was just a story." Upon further inquiry, she revealed that the stone not only wasn't "magic," but that she had stolen it from a gift shop without our knowledge.

The second episode came just a few days ago when, suddenly realizing that Christmas season was fast approaching and correctly perceiving that she may not have behaved well enough this year to secure her place on Santa's "good" list, she decided to make a desperate political play. She whispered in my ear so that her mother couldn't hear (which told me a lot about who she thinks is the easier mark in our family) a stunning proposal to engage in a conspiracy. "Dad, how about if you lie to Santa and tell him to put me on the good list?" she suggested.

While trying to contain my laughter, I honestly didn't know whether to be horrified, proud, or a little bit of both. The younger and more idealistic/naïve version of me would have surely scolded her for concocting such a devious plan. However, instead I told her that maybe a better strategy might be to actually BE good between now and the big day when Santa is set to arrive.

Part of my revised thinking was surely impacted by my fear that on her current pace she's going to figure out the Santa scam far sooner than her mother would ever want her to. However, the principal reason for me taking a pass on scolding her was based in how I now see the world and where it is clearly going. A significant part of that view is founded on the fact that Donald Trump is now our president.

Without trying to be melodramatic, or turn into a caricature of a liberal crying "what will we tell our children?!" after Trump's win, I do see his victory as the death knell for truth as a significant value in our culture. Now, to be clear, Trump's election hardly started this fire of deceit, but it did reveal that the house of honesty has now officially been burned to the ground.

Quite simply, Trump is a pathological liar and con-artist. And yet, not only did that not prevent him from somehow winning the highest office in the land, it actually *helped* him attain it by allowing him to dupe millions of fervent supporters with self-serving fairytales, spun without even a hint of remorse or self-awareness.

This phenomenon shows no signs of stopping, or even slowing down. Trump has tweeted ridiculous and clearly absurd allegations that he would have won the popular tally if there hadn't been "millions" of illegal votes cast. That is a complete lie for which there is zero evidence or logic. And yet his supporters loved it and there is no sign that this lie, like any of the hundreds of others he has told in the last year, will have any impact on his political standing.

Why? There are three primary reasons I believe. The first is that lying (ironically, thanks in large part to the Clintons) is no longer remotely taboo in our society. In fact, it is often preferred. The second is that, in this era where feelings routinely "trump" intellect, people much prefer to hear what makes them feel good (which is usually a lie) than a truth that makes them feel bad. And thirdly, people (especially Republicans) no longer trust the mainstream media to be honest about what a lie is and what is truth, and technology now allows for everyone to create their own media bubble where only comforting "information" is ever allowed inside this "safe space."

So how can I possibly reprimand my daughter when I look at what she did through the prism of how it would work in a post-Donald Trump world and I think, "damn, that kind of thinking is likely to work out quite well for her!"? Frankly, I can't. There is no doubt in my mind that our president would have smiled broadly, patted her on the back (or butt?), and complimented her survival skills if Grace was one of his children.

As much as it pains me to admit, it is now clear that in order to best prepare my children for life in this new "post-truth" era of America, they need to be educated that a well-executed lie will beat an unpopular truth every single time. So while I won't tell her that the fix is in (so to better keep her in line for a couple of weeks), I will indeed be lying to Santa that she belongs on the "good" list this year.

Thanks Donald Trump. You have taught me so very much and you aren't even president yet. I just wish I had gotten clued into these rules about forty years ago. It's too late for me now, but hopefully not for Grace.

and subtle racism immediately following President Obama's election, as pundits scrambled to write racism's epitaph. We loved the idea of Barack and Michelle Obama as role models for our children; they were paragons of intelligence, reason, fairness, and cool. But all that glitters produces temporary blindness. Obama generation kids lived through the deportation of 2.5 million undocumented people, despite stop-gap executive measures like Deferred Action for Childhood Arrivals (DACA); the continuation of Bush-era anti-terrorism policies; the consolidation of executive authority to prosecute war; and the deployment of drones in so-called "targeted assassinations" that produced thousands of civilian casualties ("collateral damage"). We can't pretend that our cool, eloquent, empathetic black president wasn't overseeing the largest secret domestic surveillance program in U.S. history and a justice department that targeted whistleblowers while refusing to *criminally* prosecute Wall Street firms whose conduct wrecked the lives of millions of working people, or that he did not consistently sign the National Defense Authorization Act (NDAA) giving him the authority to indefinitely detain anyone in the world without due process.

To be fair, President Obama and his administration's policies are not to blame for the state of our country and the world. We have at least four decades of globalization; neoliberal attacks on the welfare state public institutions, and the poor; covert wars; and political and cultural backlash against movements for racial and gender justice. Rampant xenophobia, open misogyny and attacks on reproductive rights, a backlash against "diversity," a terrifying spike in homicides of transgender people, did not begin with the Trump campaign. This political climate has been in the making for at least three decades or more. And despite a steady right-wing turn, the dismantling of government's regulatory and protective functions, obscene income and wealth disparities, and creeping privatization of everything, the country made enormous strides under Obama in the areas of climate change, health insurance, marriage equality, women's wage equity, diplomatic relations with Cuba and Iran, among other things. From this vantage point, the United States may look like a completely different country for folks unaware of life before Obama.

But here is the rub: as liberal parents, caught like deer in the headlights, scramble to explain Trump to their kids and to themselves, my wife and I—like all black parents I know—have spent the last five years trying to explain Trayvon Martin's tragic death and why his killer walked; Mike Brown's body rotting in the streets of Ferguson for four hours, his unarmed life ended by a cop who walked; Tanisha Anderson's death at the hands of police responding to a call for help as she suffered a mental breakdown; Eric Garner's dying words as a salaried officer of the law choked him to death on camera . . . and walked. You see, we had to explain to our sons that if they played outside with toy guns they could end up like Tamir Rice, or if they dressed like ninjas and carried fake swords they could end up like Darrien Hunt. We could not bury our heads in the sand and pretend that manifestations of fascism were not already here, because every other day there was a new video documenting the murder of people who looked like our kids, mostly by people in uniform with badges—some black like them. Every day we feared for our children's lives and often instructed our older son on how to conduct himself in the presence of police. We also had to explain the protests in Ferguson, in Baltimore, in Milwaukee, and elsewhere, and why it looked like an army had descended on so many angry and grieving black people. We had to explain why the state needed armored vehicles and powerful automatic weapons and tear gas to deal with these young folks—even the rowdy ones. And my president was black and affected and said, "If I had a son, he'd look like Trayvon," and then went on to increase funding for the Byrne program, which provides money for armored vehicles, SWAT armor, surveillance drones, and helicopters to ramp up the war on drugs.

We're not the only ones who had to have "talks." Muslim, Arab, and South Asian parents have been having these kinds of talks at least since 9/11, and there has been no respite under the ongoing war on terror. Many undocumented parents teach their children how to stay safe in the shadows, while others worry endlessly for those kids who boldly choose the path of public protest over subterranean existence. Native youth have been killed by the police and incarcerated in disproportionate numbers since the colonial invasion. The struggle against the Dakota Access Pipeline at Standing Rock, North Dakota, is only the latest and most visible struggle against land dispossession, resource extraction, and the violation of sovereign rights. Imagine what it means to raise children on a reservation where the unemployment rate exceeds 60 percent, where Native women are three-and-a-half times more likely to be sexually assaulted than non-Native women, where over one-fifth of the children suffer from post-traumatic stress disorder.

In other words, many of the liberals who now face an existential crisis with Trump's election never had to have these conversations. They never had to fear the state. Buying a casket for their seventeen-year-old, having a backup plan in case a parent is deported, taking a bus to visit a relative in prison, shaving one's beard or removing one's hijab or hiding a Koran—these are not the concerns of most liberal-oriented white families. And yet, they should have been. These were just a few of the signs of what has been a global shift toward authoritarianism, and the dramatic rise in civil disobedience—from Occupy to the Dreamers to Black Lives Matter—both exposed and hastened the crisis that produced Trump.

So for me the question is not how do we talk to our children about Trump? but how do we teach our children about our history—in the United States and the world? We never should have allowed our children to accept the myth that we live in a functioning democracy. Before discussing Russian hacking, we need to teach our kids about the Voting Rights Act—why we need it, the movement that made it possible, and how rich people and conservative justices succeeded in gutting its main provisions. They need to understand that Trump's election depended in part on a concerted campaign to weaken democracy through the use of voter ID laws, the elimination of Sunday voting, and schemes, such as the Interstate Voter Registration Crosscheck Program, that suppress mainly young and elderly voters and voters of color.

Most importantly, we have to begin to tell the truth about the *anti-democratic* origins of our political system, for ultimately the crises facing our democracy are endemic and can be traced back not only to the eighteenth century but to its vaunted Greco-Roman roots. Blasphemy, you say? Next time your kid is assigned Plato's *The Republic*, read along. Its clear anti-democratic strain, which not only reconciles slavery in the Republic but invents a theory of enlightened governance that excludes the popular classes, served as a model for the so-called Founding Fathers. The Founders, with few exceptions, treated captive Africans as property and did not entrust those without property with the vote. James Madison positively described his new country as an "oligarchy," insisting that land ownership had to be a requirement for participation in the body politic "as to protect the minority of the opulent against the majority." The result, besides property requirements for voting, was the electoral college. For some proponents, the electoral college served as the enlightened check against the threat of an ignorant populace backing a demagogue as president. But it also guaranteed a proslavery White House. Basic to the college's architecture was the Three-Fifths Compromise, or the rule that congressional representation in the slave states would be apportioned by counting the white population along with three out of five enslaved people. The number of electors was to be equal to the number of representatives and senators from each state. This gave the slaveholding South an edge in presidential elections compared to other states, and that advantage lasted well after slavery ended since the vast majority of black Southerners were disfranchised after Reconstruction. Ironically, critics of the electoral college who believe Clinton should be president based on the popular vote tried to invoke Alexander Hamilton's idea of the "conscientious" elector who will buck party affiliation in order to make the enlightened choice. But what does this say to our kids? That an anti-democratic institution can be wielded to ensure a democratic outcome. It is the sort of move that reinforces the myth of American democracy's singular genius while excluding forms of democracy that are not "representative." Our kids may know about the three branches of government, checks and balances, or how bills become laws, but what do they know about "direct democracy" (e.g., the Occupy Movement, the People's Assemblies in Jackson, Mississippi, participatory budgeting, etc.)?

For most "progressive" parents, teaching our kids about origins of our country, rooted in slavery, genocide, dispossession, patriarchy, and class rule, is hardly a revelation. It is even taught in many high-priced private schools. But this is not the whole story. We have inherited a rich democratic tradition, but it has existed largely outside the halls of government. The story of our democracy is the story of the most vulnerable, the despised, the dispossessed, and disrespected building social movements to *expand* democracy's horizons. In the nineteenth century it was the abolitionists, women suffragists, free labor advocates, and enslaved people themselves whose struggles to expand democracy and end all forms of bondage that created the political and social crisis that led to the Civil War. Reconstruction was the attempt to bring their vision of democracy to the state, but it was defeated by forces that wanted to make America great again by returning to the days when white men were masters, or at least believed as much. And yet, even the white supremacists could not erase the 13th, 14th, and 15th amendments to the Constitution—the scaffolding upon which new democratic movements were built in the twentienth century. These movements, not Jefferson or Madison or Hamilton, introduced equal rights to our democratic practice and continued to fight for these principles. Our failure to understand that movements matter partly explains why so many grown people—let alone our children—feel helpless and distraught in the face of Trumpism. We believe only the powerful have the power to enact change; that democracy is about choosing the right people to make the right decisions on our behalf. By reducing social movements to periodic marches on Washington or signing yet another MoveOn.org petition, we have trouble recognizing our capacity as agents of change. Ironically, our kids need to understand what the children of Trump supporters already know: that they hold the destiny of our country in their hands. They/we are the ones to widen the demos, to end racism, sexism, homophobia, and state-sanctioned violence, to stop caging people, to save the planet from rapacious capitalists, to end war and poverty and an economic system in which sixty-two people own as much wealth as half the world.

Of course, it is difficult to see how movements matter when the media depicts Occupy as a commune of disaffected, over-privileged young people out of touch with "real America," Greenpeace as "eco-terrorists," Black Lives Matter as cop-hating thugs, and politics as a kind of celebrity death match. It is widely known that Democratic contender Bernie Sanders spoke frequently about real issues and yet experienced a media blackout. Donald Trump drew coverage for every idiotic and nonsensical thing he said. Our kids are growing up in a weird, corporate media environment in which politics is reduced to gossip, tweets, and the inane opinions of pundits. Issues, policy, even truth, are casualties of the new media regime. I suppose this makes sense in a Manichean world of good vs. evil, but the world we see on our various screens is not the world in which we live. The fact that we are still talking about Donald J. Trump, the man, as if he is *the problem* rather than a *symptom* of a deeper set of structural issues is further evidence of the bankruptcy of our political discourse.

If we wish to break from the media circus of ignorance and restore our children's confidence in politics and the future, we need to do a much better job of teaching them about how the world works—and that includes understanding Trump's supporters and *their* children. How kids nurtured in a liberal, multicultural educational environment learn about the world explains a great deal about why they were caught off guard and why they came to fear and despise Trump. Our kids are taught to celebrate and "tolerate" difference, but rarely do they examine how difference is produced. They are taught to cherish equality, to disdain inequality, but never how inequality is produced. Case in point: Literally, as I write these final words, my fourteen-year-old son is in another room wrestling with his English assignment critiquing Disney movies for the way they distort history and traffic in racist and sexist stereotypes. One of the questions in the prompt asks, "Do you think Disney movies are dangerous for children?" I asked him to think beyond the content of films like *Aladdin* and *Pocahontas* and *Lion King*, and consider the entire edifice that generates desire to consume these films—that is to say, the multibillion-dollar industry comprised of theme parks, toys, pajamas, shirts, caps, and countless other items. And then we looked for the source of these commodities—over the years, Disney products have been manufactured in sweatshops in Haiti, China, and Bangladesh, where some of the workers are under age and earn a few cents an hour. Suddenly the question of whether Disney movies are "dangerous" for children took on an entirely different valence. In short, how people experience and comprehend the hidden processes of the global economy may tell us something about why Trumps are popping up all over the world and what we have to do about it.

Whatever we do, I know we have to do a better job of teaching our children, of raising politically savvy, intelligent kids who understand the dangerous world that might be new to some but old to the rest of us. After all, when Trump and his ilk are gone, many of us will still have reason to fear.

Trump Is a Great Storyteller. We Need to Be Better.

Viet Thanh Nguyen

Viet Thanh Nguyen is the Pulitzer Prize–winning author of The Sympathizer *and the Aerol Chair of English and Professor of American Studies and Ethnicity at the University of Southern California.*

MY SON IS THREE YEARS OLD. EVERY MORNING AND EVENING I READ to him. I love the joy he takes in learning new words, immersing himself in stories, seeing himself as the characters, and acquiring a moral and ethical sense. He lives in a fictional world of good and bad, of threat and rescue, of the choice between doing good or doing harm.

In Harrisburg, Pa., of the mid-1970s, I was a refugee and the child of refugees who had fled Vietnam. My parents had neither the time nor the ability to read to me in English. So I took refuge in the local public library. It became my safe space and books my constant companion.

I imagined myself amid the wonders of Manhattan, the bucolic splendor of Midwestern farms, the stirring and dreadful times of the American Revolution and Civil War. Even if there was no one who looked like me or had a name like mine, through these stories, I became an American.

As I remembered this during our presidential election, what became clear to me was that the contest for our American identity wasn't strictly a political affair. It is also a matter of storytelling. Those who seek to lead our country must persuade the people through their ability to tell a story about who we are, where we have been, and where we are going. The struggle over the direction of our country is also a fight over whose words will win and whose images will ignite the collective imagination.

Donald J. Trump won barely, and by the grace of the Electoral College. His voters responded to his call to "Make America Great Again," referring to a past when jobs were more plentiful, incomes more stable and politicians more bold.

That kind of nostalgia is powerful and visceral, but it's hard to ignore the subtext. America of the golden age, if it ever existed, kept women out of the workplace, segregated and exploited minorities, and restricted immigration by race.

It's hardly surprising that the population of much of the literary world is terrified by Mr. Trump's vision of good-versus-evil, us-against-them. At the recent National Book Awards and Dayton Literary Peace Prizes, most of the speeches proclaimed opposition to the values that Mr. Trump espoused.

That opposition isn't just political but literary: His story contradicts the idea of literature itself. Great literature cannot exist if it is based on hate, fear, division, exclusion, scapegoating or the use of injustice. Bad literature and demagogues, on the other hand, exploit these very things, and they do so through telling the kind of demonizing stories good literary writers reject.

The cast of "Hamilton" sought to remind Mike Pence, the vice president-elect, of this when he attended the show recently, imploring him directly to defend American diversity. When an offended Mr.

Trump tweeted that the theater "must always be a safe and special place," he missed their point: America itself should be a safe and special place.

Part of the fault is ours; too many writers are removed from the world of our readers. After my novel, *The Sympathizer*, was published, I would get letters from people who accused me of being "ungrateful" to the United States. The places where the book was most popular were the Northeast, West Coast and big cities. A vast section of rural Americans in the Deep South, heartland and North were not buying the book.

The day before the presidential election, an obscure novelist attacked me on Twitter. I was "NOT an American author (born in Vietnam)." As for my Pulitzer, it was "An American prize that shuns the real America. We long for the Great American Novel. When?"

Despite that criticism, this election reminds me of the necessity of my vocation. Good writers cannot write honestly if they are incapable of imagining what it is that another feels, thinks and sees. Through identifying with characters and people who are nothing like us, through destroying the walls between ourselves and others, the people who love words—both writers and readers—strive to understand others and break down the boundaries that separate us.

It's an ethos summed up by the novelist Colson Whitehead in his acceptance speech at the National Book Awards last month: "Be kind to everybody. Make art. And fight the power."

After election night, during which my partner, my graduate students and I drank two bottles of Scotch, I renewed my commitment to fight the power. That was always my mission. I was thinking of it when I named my son Ellison, after the novelist Ralph Waldo Ellison, himself named after the philosopher Ralph Waldo Emerson. Making my son a part of this lineage, I wanted him to understand the basic paradox at the heart of literature and philosophy: Even as each of us is solitary as a reader or a writer, we are reminded of our shared humanity and our inhumanity.

My son need not become a writer, but he will become a storyteller. We are all storytellers of our own lives, of our American identities. I want my son to rise to the challenge of fighting to determine which stories will define our America. That's the choice between building walls and opening hearts. Rather than making America great again, we should help America love again.

Talking to Kids About Trump's Victory

Adam Gopnik

Adam Gopnik is a staff writer for the New Yorker.

SOMEONE ASKED ME THIS MORNING TO SAY SOMETHING ABOUT TALK-ing to kids in this time of crisis. Indeed, Van Jones, speaking last night on CNN, as our own Brexitish disaster was unfolding, spoke passionately about the perils of this Wednesday morning's breakfast: What do you say to kids when a man whom they have been (rightly) brought up to regard as a monstrous figure is suddenly the president we have? I have been unstinting in my own view of the perils of Trumpism, and will remain so. But I also believe that the comings and goings of politics and political actions in our lives must not be allowed to dominate our daily existence—and that if we struggle to emphasize to our children the necessities of community, ongoing life, daily pleasures, and shared enterprises, although we may not defeat the ogres of history, we can hope to remain who we are in their face.

I went for a long walk late last night with my seventeen-year-old daughter, and noted that she felt better when she turned back, inevitably, to her cell phone and its firecracker explosions of distraught emotion from her circle. Connection, even connection in pain and dismay, is the one balm for trauma of any kind. Kids need to be reminded that those connections remain benign, no matter how frightening the images on the screen (or the panic in their parents' eyes) may be. We owe it to them not to react hyper-emotionally, even while we make an effort not to under-react intellectually—to pretend that this is just another election. Many of us learned the painful lesson of 9/11, that panic is friend only to our fears.

We teach our children history, and the history that many of them have learned in the past decade or so, at American schools and colleges, is, perhaps, unrealistic in remaining unduly progressive in tone. They learn about the brave path of the slaves' fight for freedom, about the rise of feminism, and with these lessons they learn to be rigorously skeptical of the patriarchy—without necessarily seeing that the patriarchy survives, enraged. The strangest element of this sad time is surely that our departing president, a model of eloquence and reason, is leaving office with a successful record and a high approval rating. How Trump's strange rise and Obama's high rating can have coincided in the same moment will remain one of the permanent conundrums of our history.

The lesson of history—one of them, anyway—is that there is no one-way arrow in it, that tragedy lurks around every corner, that the iceberg is there even as the mighty Titanic sails out, unsinkable. Having a tragic view of life is compatible with having a positive view of our worldly duties. This is a big and abstract thought to share with children, of course, and perhaps, like so many like it, it is teachable only as a pained—at this moment, acutely pained—daily practice.

Part Two

How You Explain This to Your Kids: Dr. Ava Siegler Offers Her Best Advice

This part of the book is written for parents who are raising children in Donald Trump's America.

In the first section, I explore different developmental stages in children and talk about how you can help them develop empathy, self-regard, self-control, and morality—civilizing characteristics that will ensure that they develop into responsible adults and good citizens, at a time when these characteristics are not displayed by members of the Trump administration.

The second section addresses specific threats against different kinds of families and children that have emerged in the Age of Trump, and discusses some ways to protect your children from these threats. I use the issues raised by the personal essays in the first part of this book as a springboard for this discussion. Of course, there are many other kinds of families who are not explicitly represented in these essays, but have also been deeply affected by Trump's policies and personality—families of veterans and activists, atheist families, etc. Families with children who are in conflict over their gender identity or parents who are already raising children who identify themselves as transgender or queer are at risk, as are families with mentally, emotionally, or physically disabled children.

While it was not possible to address every kind of family situation specifically, I hope that the information about child development, how to talk to kids, and the creation of "reparative narratives"—the subject of the third section—will be of use to *all* families in these troubled times.

A final section addresses the topic of how and when to involve kids in social activism.

Raising Civilized Children in an Uncivilized World

BE NICE!
> —*Sign held by a two-year-old girl, Women's March,*
> *January 21, 2017*

The Voice of Conscience and the Civilizing Emotion of Guilt

From their children's infancy onward, parents set limits, highlight inappropriate behaviors, and help to distinguish what is right and wrong, good and bad, safe and dangerous. This aspect of your child's education will need special attention during Trump's presidency because President Trump reveals what we would call "bad character": he's a bully, he's crass, he pathologically lies, he's vitriolic, and he's vindictive. We don't want our children modeling this behavior.

What is "good character"? How is it formed? Helping your child develop good character means nourishing the moral sense of right and wrong that we call the voice of conscience, developing a capacity for empathy (the ability to understand someone else's point of view, feel what another is feeling, and imagine what it's like to be someone else), constructing a positive and realistic sense of self-regard (neither self-destructive and self-demeaning, nor self-aggrandizing and grandiose), and helping your child bring his aggressive impulses (which are completely natural in a two-year-old but inappropriate in a seventy-year-old) under his own control (developing "self-control").

By the time he's five, your child has developed the voice of conscience. Let's look at how this happens. At first, the direction is external—you tell your toddler what he may and may not do: "No, don't touch that!" Then, little by little, your child begins to internalize your directions and control his impulses, thoughts, and feelings on his own. Many children struggle with this developmental task; many teenagers grapple with their desires versus their conscience, and many adults still have difficulty distinguishing between what's right and what's wrong. This is completely normal. There are many shades of grey that lie between black and white.

But there are some adults who appear to have no conscience at all. They are likely to break the law or commit violent crimes, or run a Ponzi scheme to trick people out of their money, or cheat their employees. Unfortunately, adults without conscience are able to take their place in all walks of our society, often without detection or punishment. (In fact, their ruthlessness is often rewarded by financial success.) A child without a conscience is tragic, but an adult without a conscience is terrifying. We need to particularly ensure that our children are guided by conscience in these morally bankrupt times.

When your child ignores the voice of his conscience, he feels guilty. Guilt can develop only if your child internalizes your own moral regulations. It is an ordinary part of growing up. Picture a three-year-old, a five-year-old, and a seven-year-old left in an empty room with a jar full of candy. The mother of each admonishes, "Don't eat the candy!" as she leaves the room. The three-year-old, after waiting a bit, will happily consume the candy, as the adult prohibition, not yet internalized, quickly fades from his memory. The five-year-old might say to herself, "No, no, don't eat the candy," but after a while, perhaps even looking anxious, she will probably still eat some candy. The seven-year-old, however, is already capable of listening to the voice of her conscience, and worried about disapproval, so taking a piece of candy will elicit guilt, her normal underlying apprehension about doing the right thing.

While guilt often gets a bad name, it is actually one of our most significant "civilizing emotions." The trick is to strengthen your child's conscience while still preserving her spirit, will, and autonomy. Guilt is a necessary part of our social life, but too much guilt can cripple your child's spirit, and too little can leave him unable to tell right from wrong. A person who feels no guilt always acts out of self-interest. And a person who is never remorseful feels justified in whatever he chooses to do, and never sees the need to apologize. The thousands of voters who appear at town halls to confront their congressmen and shout "Shame on You! Shame on You!" are trying to mobilize a sense of guilt in them.

Failures of Conscience: Lying, Boasting, Bullying, and Blaming

Once the voice of conscience is established and your child feels guilty when she's done something wrong, the wish to escape disapproval becomes stronger. Sometimes it becomes so strong that your child will resort to lying to escape an unpleasant situation. Lying is widespread among children as well as among adults. We all lie for many reasons— to avoid detection, to protect another from a harsh truth, to conceal information, to escape responsibilities, to avoid punishment, to control others, to protect self-regard, to exaggerate self-worth. The fact that children lie from time to time doesn't make them liars, it makes them human. But persistent lying indicates a deeper emotional disturbance, and lying in the face of a blatant fact can be delusional. A person with delusions is no longer in touch with reality. Instead, he has created his own reality and occupies it, without regard for the truth.

Don't confuse childhood lies and their various meanings with Trump's pathological lies. They represent very different behaviors. Nevertheless, in this political climate, you need to be alert to your child's lies (for example, "I don't have any homework."). First, try to understand the reasons for the lie: Is he having trouble in school? Does he feel inadequate? Is there something else he wants to do (watch a show, see a friend)? Then explain to him that you don't ever want him to lie to you. *Sound serious!* Go on to say if he lies, you can't trust anything he says, and that would be awful for both of you. Imagine if you lied to him or promised him things that you never gave to him. Or even worse, he could be in real trouble and you wouldn't believe him, like the story of "The Boy Who Cried Wolf."

Remember that for a very young child (under seven years old) the ability to distinguish between fact and fantasy is often blurred, and their desires can easily overpower the truth.

- Correct your young child's "lies" by stating, for example, "I know you *wish* you owned a puppy, but we don't, so you can't tell Lily that you have a puppy at home, because it isn't true."

Try to sharpen a young child's understanding of what's true and what's not true by playing games like "True or False?" and label her "lies" as "pretending" or "make-believe," which she will understand. Children this age may insist on maintaining their fantasy even in the face of your correction and disapproval. Don't get punitive! Simply repeat, "I know you wish you had a puppy, but we don't. That's just pretending."

For older, school-aged children who are now capable of following rules and are interested in fairness, you need to directly confront lying and monitor your child's behavior. Lying is tempting; interfere with her ability to get away with it, or she will lose respect for you and herself.

- "You told me that you finished your project for school, but your teacher emailed me to say that you didn't hand it in. When you don't tell the truth you are the one who gets hurt. People don't trust you. Both your teacher and I are upset with you for lying. Until I know you can be trusted again I've arranged to have your teacher email me your work assignments every night."

Teenagers are trying to live a private life without you; that's their job—to separate from their parents and attach to their peers during adolescence. When a teenager lies (and they often evade the truth), it's usually to protect herself, her friends, and her social life from your scrutiny. Some lying of this sort is normal at this age because it's in the service of practicing independence. But of course, you need to keep an eye on lies that could result in your teenager placing herself in danger. Particularly as teenagers begin to experiment with adult behaviors (smoking, sex, drugs), they are likely to lie by omission. When caught, they can become angry and defensive, and even try to justify their lies: "No other parents care about a chaperone at the party; I'm not a baby"; "I didn't want you to worry, so I didn't tell you"; "My phone was in my pocket, so I didn't see your text"; or even, "President Trump lies all the time, so what's the big deal?"

- Make it clear to your teen that lying is unacceptable to you— you don't care if her friends lie or Trump lies, or anybody lies—you expect her to tell you the truth.

- The more your teenager trusts you and the more you keep a line of communication open with her, particularly about risky behaviors, the less she is likely to lie to you.
- Make sure she knows that you'll punish her much less if she tells the truth than if she lies and you find out about it later.

As far as Trump's lies, if you watch the news, be sure to point them out ("That's not true—immigrants are not terrorists") and also distinguish between real facts and Trump's "alternative facts," or between "real news" and "fake news" for your child. Trump's rhetoric is very persuasive because he says the same thing over and over again in simple words and a loud voice. (Children particularly respond to adults who sound powerful and authoritative.)

In his essay, John Ziegler expresses his disillusion about the current state of truth in our society. He believes that Trump's victory is a "death knell for truth as a significant value in our culture." He talks about the fact that he was raised to believe that "honesty is the best policy," but that he's learned in the course of his life that "this premise is usually false." As a parent, he is torn by his uneasiness about his four-year-old daughter's resort to lying, but he is also reluctant to scold her: perhaps her lies are adaptive in our new Trumpian society?

We can all understand his despair, but Trump's pathological lying has actually *heightened* the significance of the truth for millions of people. It has highlighted the importance of the difference between fact and fiction, and underscored the power of trust in human affairs. Fact-checking has taken on new meaning, as newspapers now have entire pages devoted to untangling Trump's lies from the truth, and reporters and television commentators constantly challenge his words. The *New York Times* even published a special supplement describing that "the truth is more important now than ever," listing sixteen reasons why this is so.[1]

Do not relinquish your values no matter how disillusioned you feel. We owe it to our children to discuss what's true and what's not, or else we undermine the development of the voice of conscience, and their morality as citizens of the world. Trump's pathological lying is often his attempt to exaggerate his self-worth. He is shamelessly boastful and grandiose. Not a day goes by that Trump doesn't lie about manifestly untrue things—the size of the crowds at his inauguration, his electoral victory, the state of the economy, the level of crime in our inner cities.

One of the ways Trump tries to feel big is to make someone else feel small. Trump cannot seem to have a conversation in which he does not inflate and boast about himself while demeaning another person's characteristics. We've seen him taunt his opponents during the election ("Lying Ted," "Crooked Hillary," "Little Marco," etc.), and he has continued this particular brand of nastiness into his presidency, mocking reporters, demeaning judges, and attacking critics. Molly Knefel, a teacher in the Bronx (whose students are either immigrants or children of immigrants), makes the point in her essay that Donald Trump "speaks in threats that a seven-year-old can understand." She notes that children "are quoting Trump to bully one another." This identification with Trump can distort your child's development (it's called "identification with the aggressor"). If you see it in your child, criticize it and correct it: "You know we feel President Trump is a bully. Under no condition will we let you grow up to be mean like he is."

In the past decade, there has been a heightened awareness of how dangerous bullying can be, particularly cyber-bullying, which has even caused teenagers to attempt suicide. But in these times, bullying is going to be very much with us. If your child is being bullied, you need to find out as much as possible about the circumstances. Often, children who do not conform to some "norm" are singled out by bullies. Your child may be smaller or thinner or plumper or more timid than other kids, leaving her vulnerable to bullies. Effeminate boys are also often targeted, as are children struggling with conflicts over gender identity. Bullying becomes more dangerous as your child moves into adolescence. In this Trumpian atmosphere, aggression directed toward racial and religious differences has sharply increased, so many children of different races and religions are also more likely to be targeted.

School can be a sanctuary or a hotbed of hostility. Tangible manifestations of difference, like wearing a hijab or a yarmulke, will draw hostility from children who have been taught to be intolerant of differences. You need to decide what to do when protecting your children may be in conflict with your religious beliefs. Some children may refuse to wear a hijab or a yarmulke to a secular school, while others will wear it proudly. (A lot depends upon how many children in the school will also be wearing visible religious garb.) School is where your children spend most of their day.

- Make sure the school your child goes to is willing to protect them.
- Speak to school officials about their policies regarding bullying and discrimination.
- Ask that a teacher or guidance counselor be designated as your child's "safe adult."

You also need to talk with your children about *their* level of comfort maintaining *your* religious observances. If you feel strongly that your children need to be strictly raised with orthodox religious traditions and beliefs, one option would be to enroll them in a religious school that can support them.

Racial differences, however, cannot be taken off and on like religious garb, and the long history of racial prejudice in this country has always required parents of black and brown children to prepare them for antagonism.

- Encourage your children to report bullying to you.
- Watch for changes in your child's mood. A child's reluctance to attend school can often reveal distress within the school setting.
- If your children are being racially bullied in school (through words or deeds), immediately contact school authorities and insist that a plan be put in place to help keep your children safe.

Here are some tips to tell your children:

- Avoid and ignore a bully; don't engage.
- Stick with your friends; there's safety in numbers.
- Avoid neighborhoods that feel or appear unsafe.

As well as protecting your child and securing his safety in school, you need to help strengthen your child in as many ways as possible. Improving his self-esteem through realistic encouragement of his efforts, and confirming his developing identity by admiring his accomplishments, can build his character. Your children can also increase their confidence by strengthening their bodies. It's helpful for kids who feel threatened to study martial arts or boxing or judo—not because they're going to use these skills on the bully, but because it helps them feel more competent and less afraid.

Children who are struggling to define their gender identity are often at high risk for hostility and aggression from others. By the time your gender-conflicted child is six or seven, the wish to occupy another body that better represents their internal sense of themselves may be revealed; boys want to dress like girls and play with girls' toys, and girls want to dress like boys and do things boys do. When this idea becomes compelling and dominates your child's life, he or she is likely to be a transgender child. Don't confuse this with girls who are "tomboys" or just have interests that are similar to boys' interests, or with boys who don't like aggressive sports or fighting and instead like to draw or cook or read. This is also different from homosexuality, which is defined by the wish/need to love someone of the same sex, and is usually revealed in preadolescence or adolescence, when sexual intimacy is first contemplated.

Protecting a transgender child is difficult and complicated. You need to find the right school, register your child in the name she or he wishes to be called, and talk to school authorities about gaining access to bathrooms that match his or her gender identity—something that the Trump administration is no longer willing to protect. (It's also crucial to seek out legal help as it becomes necessary along your child's path.) Explore your own feelings as well as your child's feelings about this gender shift, and help your child to deal with the reactions of other people, even family members who may be confused and feel a sense of loss of the child they knew. Remember, *you* are your transgender child's most important support, but you need support too, so try to connect with other parents who are coping with this same issue. Transgender children frequently feel depressed and isolated until they can be the gender they want to be, so psychological support services with therapists who specialize in these problems can be crucial. Medical consultation surrounding issues including suppressing your child's hormonal activity, or gender reassignment surgery, may need to be considered, as well.

Tell your transgender child:

- "What's most important to us is that you are able to *be* who you feel you *are*. We will support you in every way we can in becoming the person you want to be."
- "Other children or adults may be anxious or even angry about you changing your identity. Just tell them, 'I am meant to be a boy/girl.'"

- "Walk away from kids who tease you or make fun of you; stick to kids who know you and like you."

Most schools have at least one bathroom designated for adults or faculty. Work with your child's school administrator to allow your child access to this bathroom if the school will not allow your child to use the student bathroom corresponding to your child's chosen identity.

If your child *is* the bully, you need to acknowledge and name the problem: "I noticed that when Sam came over and the two of you were playing, you bullied him a lot, making him do what you wanted." Children who bully others often suffer from what I call the Superman/Clark Kent syndrome. On the outside, they appear strong and even super powerful, but on the inside they are anxious and often fearful. Make sure your child understands that bullying is an unacceptable behavior and that you do not see it as a strength. Set limits and consequences for his bullying. He may need help in controlling his impulses. Teaching a bully to obey the rules of the game through sports like hockey or soccer is also useful because the team will curb his aggression. Coaches often teach cooperation and good sportsmanship and encourage team spirit. A child who is bullied needs to develop skills, and so does the child who is the bully. If your child feels competent and confident, he will neither be a bully nor be bullied.

Encouraging Empathy, Another Civilizing Emotion

It's important to teach empathy—another key "civilizing emotion"—at an early age. Even a three-year-old can be told, "You need to share these cookies with your sister. She's crying because she wants one." Or you can instruct your six-year-old, "Even though you're mad at Molly, you can't call her names; it hurts her feelings," or explain to your ten-year-old, "That man is sleeping in the street because he's poor and homeless;

let's go buy him a sandwich," or "Can you imagine how that reporter must feel, being yelled at by the president of the United States?"

By demonstrating your empathic values to your child and acting empathetically toward her, you help her to nurture her own empathic responses. As she grows, her capacity for empathy grows. Having empathy for others will eventually enable her to serve as a valuable member of society. No matter what work she chooses, empathy will help her get along and get ahead. A child without the capacity for empathy is crippled in all of his social and emotional relationships. He doesn't understand other people's thoughts or feelings, he is unable to feel love for another, and he is likely to be perceived as heartless, selfish, or disconnected.

Remember, too, that the absence of empathy underlies all forms of bigotry and hatred. It permits the cruelties of war, the enslavement of peoples, the torture of prisoners, and genocide. In order to destroy someone, you must first feel alienated from him, to see him as less than you, or even less than human. If you have a capacity for empathy, you cannot reach this state of alienation because you can always feel another's pain. An empathic child is a kind child, a considerate child, and a loving child. We need these kinds of children in today's world more than ever.

Creating Realistic Self-Regard

By the time your child is of school age she will have begun the process of consolidating her sense of self—the self she has created and now hopes the world will welcome. This self has accumulated in layers over all the years your child has lived—and even before her birth, because the bottom layer is your child's biological beginnings. We know that children bring certain temperamental characteristics with them into the world. There are calm, placid babies; restless, sensitive babies; alert, active babies. As parents react and respond to their baby's temperament, they shape and are shaped by their baby's emerging personality.

The self is anchored in a wide array of behaviors that characterize your child's way of being in the world. With the emergence of a continuous sense of self, self-esteem (good feelings about the self), self-doubt (uncertain feelings about the self), and self-contempt (bad feelings about the self) are possible. Self-regard regulation (the ability to keep up good feelings about yourself when bad things are happening to you) now becomes a crucial developmental objective.

When your child's good feelings are undermined—by hearing that President Trump doesn't like Mexicans, or learning that he's enforcing a ban against immigrants or deporting undocumented residents, or just hearing the president's escalated anger against his opponents—self-doubt gets raised. "I'm such a loser," your child may think, or "Nobody likes me." We feel the same sense of shame, dread, and fear in our teen years when we experience the taunting of a Trump supporter or we overhear anti-Semitic or anti-black comments. As adults, when we get profiled and pulled over by a cop or aren't promoted when it was deserved, we feel bad about ourselves. Maintenance of a good sense of self in the face of bad times is critical to your child's emotional health.

These are bad times. Be aware that President Trump's hostile criticisms of ethnic and religious groups, his contempt for women, his bullying, and his racism have put pressure on our children to continue to feel good about themselves. It makes our job as parents harder.

Parents often think they are building up a child's self-esteem by telling her how great she is, how talented she is, how wonderful she is, and how special she is. But true self-esteem must come from the *self*, not from *others*. Your child needs to feel good about what she does because she recognizes the efforts she makes and can appreciate her own accomplishments. Praise the *process*, not the *product* ("I can see you worked really hard on that drawing. I love the colors you chose; you must feel really good about it," rather than "That's the most beautiful drawing I've ever seen! You're a great artist! You are so talented!"). The latter approach will only make your child feel anxious that she can never keep up this level of accomplishment, and she will focus her attention on *being* an artist rather than on *becoming* an artist.

In this Age of Trump, a child's self-esteem also needs to be shielded from Trump's angry criticisms of others. Be sure to emphasize that Trump's criticality reflects badly on him; it's his hostile personality. Try to deprive his words of power. Humor is a good way to do this. (Think about the *Saturday Night Live* parodies of Trump and his followers and make sure your older children and teenagers see them. Showing the absurdity of Trump's behavior diminishes his influence.) Satire is, of course, a way to deflate the extreme positions of either the right or the left. But in this Trumpian climate, the two sides cannot be considered equal. We might mock Rachel Maddow because she makes a big deal about two pages of Trump's tax returns, but we mock President Trump because we believe he is dangerous.

Trump's lying and bullying and boasting are psychologically connected; they reinforce each other. He also relies on a defense that psychologists call "projection," or "externalizing blame." Nothing is ever his responsibility; it's always someone else's fault. His message is, "I'm great and you're not," and "If there's anything wrong, you're to blame." These are all traits we do not want to see our children imitate or develop: lying, name-calling, bullying, boastfulness, and blaming others.

Building Self-Control

We're all capable of anger and hate as well as affection and love. It is a parent's job to help a child to modulate anger, and to control and transform hostile impulses so that he can have friends, attend school, and become a member of society. We try to civilize our children by encouraging *assertion* while curtailing *aggression*.

Our society is very ambivalent about the uses and abuses of aggression. On the one hand, we try to teach our kids to cooperate with each other; on the other hand, we encourage competition. We profess to be against violence, but we have unrestricted access to guns, and the highest incidence of murder among the civilized countries of the Western world. We think of ourselves as peace-loving, yet we engage in many wars. No wonder we can't decide as parents whether we want to raise assertive, self-centered achievers or cooperative, selfless, good Samaritans! We all want our children to be successful, yet the qualities emphasized in the climb to the top may be qualities we don't like to live with—particularly in our own families.

The key for parents is finding a way to encourage your kid's *assertion* (the ability to speak up and speak out) and discourage your child's *aggression*. This is more important than ever now as the country embarks upon a massive resistance to an unusually aggressive president. We must remain assertive, yet peaceful in order to remain effective.

Recall Senator Mitch McConnell silencing Senator Elizabeth Warren on the Senate floor as she was reading Coretta Scott King's letter in opposition to Senator Jeff Sessions. While previously permitting all sorts of aggressive exchanges among male senators (Senator Lindsey Graham wished that Senator Ted Cruz would die on the Senate floor), McConnell applied a double standard to Senator Warren, invoking a seldom-enforced prohibition against speaking ill of another. He forbade Elizabeth Warren to continue, stating, "She was warned. She was given an explanation. Nevertheless, she persisted." Instead of cowering and feeling chastened, women all over the country have rallied to support Senator Warren. She persisted. Senator Warren is an assertive woman. President Trump, with his petulance, his rages, his vindictiveness, and his insults, is an aggressive man. We must make this distinction for our children.

As parents, one of the most difficult things we have to contend with under Trump's presidency is his widespread use and abuse of aggression to intimidate and control others. During his candidacy we saw this emerge among his supporters at his rallies, who became increasingly fired up, responding to Trump's lack of constraint and his intentional rabble-rousing (and Trump has continued to hold these rallies into his presidency). When we talked about the development of your child's sense of self, one of the things we emphasized was the need for self-control. How many times do you say to your kids, "Use your words, not your hands!" or tell them, "When you say you hate Margaret, that's a very strong word. Maybe it would be better to say you don't like what Margaret did."

In his essay, David Valdes Greenwood describes what makes Trump's presidency so dangerous: President Trump "has surely granted permission for people to not just indulge their worst thoughts, but to absolutely revel in them. He stoked a fire in people who have grown tired of making the effort to extend civility and human decency to those not like them. What was once a goading whisper has become the roar of the crowd." These words remind us that the parameters of civilized behavior exist for a reason. We all have the potential for hatred and aggression within us, but in the course of our development we learn to modulate and restrain these impulses in order to live in peace and harmony with our fellow citizens. (Freud discusses this human effort in his famous book *Civilization and Its Discontents*.) President Trump has altered these parameters and licensed the expression of all sorts of aggression; he is uncivilized.

Ordinarily, parents correct aggression in their children by the time they are toddlers and guide them toward more appropriate behavior. As the years of Trump's presidency unfold, we are going to need to pay special attention to strengthening our children's self-control. Not only does this mean drawing upon conscience and empathy and your child's sense of self, it's also going to mean calling out evidence of aggression in the media, in the schools, and in your life.

The untrammeled nastiness, hostility, and vindictiveness that we see in politics these days can have a lasting effect upon our children. Children look up to the adults around them to learn clues about human behavior. If their teacher is mean to one of their friends, if the policeman on your block threatens your neighbors, or if the members of your government treat each other in contemptuous and offensive ways, the message given to your child is that aggression is permissible or even admired. We've worked as a civilization for thousands of years to move away from the cruel and brutish practices of the generations before us, only to find ourselves in an unprecedented return to more primitive times. *Manners matter; ethics matter; customs matter.* Restraint binds our civilization, and President Trump seems intent on unbinding it.

One problem for those of us who oppose Trump's uncivil behavior is that often we are tempted to "fight fire with fire." Remember, it's hard to quash tyranny without becoming tyrannical yourself. Tell your children, "Even wars have conventions that govern them. We have to remain human beings. Even if we hate our enemies and believe that they don't deserve to live, soldiers are not permitted to torture them. It destroys the very principles we live by in a democracy." If you see behavior in your child that is modeled after Trump and his followers, be sure to "nip it in the bud." For example, if your school-aged child is not a Trump supporter and has cursed at his friend who is, you need to tell him:

- "I know you're angry with Jonathan because he likes Trump and you don't, but you can't call him names and curse at him, because that just makes you like Trump."
- "You need to tell Jonathan you don't agree with him, and you're angry that he's supporting someone who you feel is hurting our country. That's what we expect of you."

By paying attention to your child's development of conscience, empathy, and sense of self, as well as modulating their aggression, you can still raise a civilized child in what now appears to be our increasingly uncivilized world.

Protecting Your Children in the Trump Era

The New Normal Is Insane.
—Sign on "Not My President's Day,"
February 20, 2017

POLITICAL CYCLES ARE HISTORICAL. WE PROGRESS AND REGRESS. As parents we try to protect the rhythms of our children's lives against political fortune. We also try to lend our adult perspective to our children and to place political figures in their historical context. Donald Trump may be one of our most ill-prepared and dangerous presidents, but he is hardly the first to put us all at risk. Even wonderful presidents have entangled us in terrible wars.

Being a protective parent means trying to shield your child from experiences that could overwhelm her, while helping her to understand and master experiences that can help her to grow. As parents, we make these decisions on a daily basis—we try not to overprotect our kids, but we also try not to overexpose them. Disruptive intrusions in our children's lives are inevitable; we cannot protect them from the complex lives they will lead in a multiracial, multiethnic, democratic society.

But parents across the country are particularly troubled now, and for good reason. The president himself is modeling behavior that we do not want our children to absorb or imitate.

In addition, today's media- and social-media-driven world makes it harder than ever to protect our children. They are exposed to more information more quickly than ever before, and we have less parental control over this information. Also, the information itself is likely to be sparse and shallow, not expansive or deep, so our children may be less able to think things through and more likely to accept superficial explanations. (Displaying behavior we would be unhappy to see in our children, our president himself seems more interested in tweets and TV than in reading.)

As adults, we are naturally worried about President Trump's policies, but as parents we must particularly protect our kids from President Trump's character flaws. We cannot allow these to become normalized; his uncivil traits must be recognized as aberrant.

In psychology, we describe human behavior as either "ego-syntonic," meaning that a person's behavior is seen by him as an acceptable part of his personality, or "ego-alien," where the person feels that his behavior is unacceptable and he wants to change this part of his personality. Sadly, President Trump's disturbing behavior is ego-syntonic for him; he does not recognize that there is anything wrong with his character. He feels entitled and justified to be who he wants to be, say what he wants to say, and do what he wants to do, no matter the harm to others. This means that as parents we need to implement protective strategies right away.

- For younger children: Limit your younger child's exposure to President Trump's outbursts, speeches, and rallies.
- For older children: Watch the news with your older children and interpret what's going on so they are not brought under

the sway of Trump's rhetoric, which is repetitious and powerful.

- For teenagers: Engage your teenager in a discussion about
  our democracy, our constitution, and President Trump's lack
  of knowledge of and disrespect for the law.
- For all kids: Call out Trump's lies, and correct the record.

The Five Basic Fears and How President Trump Magnifies Them

Our fears define our perceptions, stimulate our senses, guide our judgments, and testify to our shared experiences. A child raised with too
much fear will cower and cringe before life's demands, but one raised
with too little fear may never survive at all. By understanding your
children's fears, you can help your kids to strengthen and grow. By
talking to your kids about their fears, you become a protective parent.

In my work with children, teenagers, and their parents, I have come
to believe that there are five basic fears we all must conquer throughout our lives—fear of the unknown, fear of being alone (or being left
alone), fears about our bodies, fears of the voice of conscience, and fears
about the self. The Trump era has heightened all five of these fears for
kids and parents: "What is President Trump going to do today?" "Will
Daddy have to go back to Mexico and leave us?" "The kids at school
said I'm a terrorist and they're gonna beat me up." "I hate Trump, but
our minister said we shouldn't keep hate in our hearts." "Why doesn't
President Trump care about gay/lesbian/transgender kids like me?"

Parents have a tricky job in the Trump era. You want to develop
a strong sense of social justice in your children and alert them to
President Trump's failings, but you also need to help your child learn
how to accommodate and compromise with others who may not feel
as you do. You must teach your children to respect the institution of

democracy even while you may not approve of our democracy's current elected head or the specifics of the system that was used to elect him. You need to try to help your kids understand differences of opinion, and to be tolerant. This means trying to understand the people who support Trump, too. Carlos Sandoval in his essay calls upon his memories and his empathy to understand "the despair created by gutted-out industrial sectors in the Midwest, the sense of abandonment in coal territory, the anxiety of family farmers we once held as our American ideal but who now can't hold on to the farm without an outside job." He points out that white America is finally realizing that they, too, feel the alienation and despair that black Americans have felt for generations.

Some of the people who support Trump may be friends or neighbors, or even members of your own family. It's hard for children to understand that people who love us can make decisions (like supporting Trump) that hurt us. When these political differences arise, you need to explain them to your children:

- "Grandpa Tony doesn't like Muslims. He thinks they're all terrorists. He's forgotten that people used to believe all Italians were in the Mafia. We don't agree with him, but we still love him, and he's still your grandpa, so let's not discuss politics with him again."
- "Aunty Nora voted for Trump, but she knows we feel he's a terrible president. Her son is a coal miner, and she feels Trump will put him back to work."
- "I can't stand another dinner with the Barretts. They talk about ways Trump is going to make America great again, and they really mean make America *white* again. They're racists, and I don't want to make any plans with them. You can see Allyson in school or she can come over to our house, but you can't go over to her house."

Your children's escalated fears, promoted by "Trump talk," can stretch your kids' limited psychological resources beyond their capacities. Viewing immigrants being taken off planes, or locked up and restrained, is particularly painful for children who themselves are immigrants. Hearing Mexicans called rapists and drug dealers is frightening to Hispanic families, and the chaotic enactment of a Muslim ban without justice or reason is extraordinarily terrifying in a country that was created on the premise of religious and cultural freedom.

Keep these suggestions in mind when you talk to your children:

- Acknowledge your child's fears; don't dismiss or deny them: "I understand why you're afraid. President Trump is so unpredictable we never know what he's going to do, and he doesn't believe in a lot of the things we believe in."
- Label your child's feelings; often children are unaware of how they feel: "I think you feel angry that there's so much talk about Trump whenever we get together with friends. It makes us all upset."
- Offer as much realistic reassurance as you can: "Even though Trump is president now, your life is going to stay the same. We're going to live in our house, and you'll go to the same school, and we'll see all our friends and family. We're not going anywhere."
- Be as honest as you can if reassurance won't work. If you and your child are undocumented immigrants, you will need to have a plan to go underground or seek refuge in a sanctuary city, which may require moving and disrupting your family's life. Emphasize for your child that you will all try to stay together. List all the people who love him and could take care of him. He will never be left alone. (That will be his deepest fear.) If your child was born here, but you were not, contact

refugee agencies. They can offer free legal advice and support to help keep your family together.

- Use your historical perspective to help your child understand Trump's presidency: "We've had very, very good presidents and very, very bad presidents before, but our country has always survived, and we're going to survive this time, too."
- Hold out hope for the future: "Trump is not a dictator even though he acts like one. We're all going to work hard to make sure he is not elected president again."

Particularly Protecting Your Girls

In his essay, Dan Kois talks about wanting to protect his kids and tell them that, "things will be fine, America is still the best, we'll have a chance to elect a woman four years from now." But he realizes that he needs to "break their hearts" and tell his nine-year-old and eleven-year-old girls the truth about half the country supporting a man like Trump. And Trump's attitude toward women *is* heartbreaking, so parents of girls must counteract his demeaning comments. Be aware that President Trump's control of and contempt for women has made it more difficult for our girls to continue to feel good about themselves. Little girls of all races and ethnicities have seen a man in the highest office of our land belittle and objectify them and their bodies. Trump's exploitative, sexualized attitude is hard to explain to girls, but you can help kids put words to this and debunk these attitudes by pointing out that, "Trump values beauty over a woman's mind or personality or education" or, "He feels entitled to molest women because he's a celebrity," and explaining why these values are wrong.

Preteen and teenage girls have a heightened awareness of their changing bodies and a sensitivity about their value as they become women. We are never going to escape the judgments of others, but the particular vulgarity of President Trump's words and deeds in relation to women exposes the worst aspects of exploitative and aggressive male behavior. Teenage girls are acutely aware of interest in and scrutiny of their bodies, particularly by old men, and alert to anyone who seems "weird" or "pervy" or just plain "disgusting."

David Valdes Greenwood, a Latino, gay dad of an African-American girl, emphasizes in his essay that, "*nothing* compares to the depths of Trump's grossness and crassness on the subject of women . . . their worth and credibility based on his scale of beauty; he boasts about how conquests bolster a man's success."

These four years will be a good time to love your girls for their whole selves, to encourage their self-regard in every aspect of their being, and to reassure them that, while some men don't respect women, most men are not like Trump. Darlena Cunha, who has eight-year-old twin girls, is horrified by Trump's treatment of women; additionally, she goes on to explain that she lives in Florida and her girls' elementary school is "Trump-leaning." For the first time, she feels cautious about protecting her children in this environment: "I was suddenly afraid of free speech." Interestingly, her daughters are already monitoring what they say and how they say it. They are sensitive to their school atmosphere.

Since the 1960s in our country, with the rise of the women's movement and the national commitment to feminism, women have advanced into all walks of life, breaking barriers as they move ahead. When I first became a psychologist, the field was dominated by men, as were medicine and law. In the past fifty years, these fields have become increasingly feminized, with women leading the way. In the financial world, represented by the statue of a charging bull on Wall Street, on International Women's Day, female artist Kristen Visbal created a bronze statue entitled *Fearless Girl* facing the bull, to indicate that women are challenging this male bastion.

Young girls and teenagers who have grown up in the Obama years and have seen the role women played in his administration, and have observed his respectful relationship to his wife and daughters, are stunned by the TV images of President Trump striding ahead, trailed by his silent wife Melania or his subservient daughter Ivanka. Teen-aged girls are outraged at being treated as objects of male desire in these Trumpian times, and millennials are shocked that their rights as women to health care, contraceptive care, and abortion seem under threat by this administration.

- Educate your children about the history of the fight for women's rights, as well as civil rights. Point out that power-ful women in all walks of life have been at the forefront of the fight against Trump's reactionary policies. Sally Yates, an assistant attorney general, blocked Trump's original immi-gration ban (and was fired for it). The only Republican sena-tors who voted against the appointment of Betsy DeVos as secretary of education, despite DeVos's lack of qualifications, were Susan Collins of Maine and Lisa Murkowski of Alaska. And the Women's March was the largest public protest in the history of the United States.
- To help your daughter retain her self-esteem and strength in the face of Trump's words and deeds, give her an historical perspective on how far women have come in this country, and reassure her that we're not going back.
- Emphasize all the heroic women who have been fighting against Trump.
- Help her to understand that the fight is not over for girls and women and that you are going to support her in every way you can.

Nicole Chung describes in her essay showing her saddened eight-year-old daughter Hillary Clinton's concession speech, "To all of the little girls who are watching this, never doubt that you are valuable and powerful and deserving of every chance and opportunity in the world to pursue and achieve your own dreams." Her daughter replies, "I'm still sad, but I feel a little better. We'll try to stop Donald Trump from doing all the bad things he wants to do. And I think there will be a woman president someday." We all hope that the pervasive misogyny we experience now will not prevent the next woman candidate from becoming president, and it's important both to condemn Trump's derogatory behavior and to nurture this hope for change in our daughters and sons today.

Special Challenges for Muslim Families

For Muslim families, suspicion and antagonism have been particularly strong since the national trauma of September 11th. This suspicion makes many Muslims fear the very government that is supposed to protect them. As Huda Al-Marashi's fourteen-year-old son puts it in her essay, "Haters gonna hate us." Samantha Schmidt, in her essay, describes one Muslim father talking about his pain and disappointment at American bigotry: "He thought he had left behind conflicts over religion in Lebanon, where sectarian tensions cast a long shadow. 'I came here and found the same things following me,' he said." Mr. Elcharfa wants his children to assimilate and become Americans. But the current anti-Muslim climate has made this difficult, and his wife feels very differently. She wants her daughters to wear the hijab and retain their customs. She encourages her daughter Zaynub to follow the prophet Muhammad and forgive the boys who taunted her in school. "We forgive," she states, "so we can always live in peace."

Trump's focus on Muslims as the enemy and his insistence on referring to radical *Islamic* terrorists has targeted and encouraged anger
among his supporters toward the Muslim community. The racial and
religious profiling that is being perpetuated extends discrimination and
persecution to many other groups, including Arabs, Sikhs, and other
South Asians, who may or may not be Muslim. White supremacists are
not distinguishing among these groups, and violence is rising.

Fears of being hated, being tormented, or being taken away are not
new. And the implementation of aggressive orders through the government, the police, the prosecutors, and the courts is not new either.
What *is* new is the blatant, shameless expression of hatred, the repudia-
tion of "political correctness," the bald justification of scapegoating of
Muslims by this president, and the sense that the government cannot
be relied upon to categorically reject citizen-on-citizen violence.

Our nation was formed by giving refuge to those fleeing persecution
in their own lands. If you are talking to your Muslim children about
President Trump's policies, try to place his hostility in an historical
context:

- "America is a strange place. On the one hand, it has always
  welcomed immigrants, but on the other, it has always re-
  sented them and felt threatened by them, too. Before there
  was anger toward Muslims, there was anger toward the Irish,
  Italians, Jews, Asians, and Hispanics. Religious and racial
  prejudice often lies just under the surface in American life,
  and under the Trump administration it has become more
  visible."

Make sure to seek out support for your family in your mosque, school, and neighborhood. Reach out to your neighbors, and make yourself and your children known to them.

It's important to directly discuss the Muslim ban with your children. Explain that the American courts struck it down but that President Trump still wants to prevent Muslims from immigrating to the United States. Point out how hundreds of thousands of Americans protested on behalf of Muslims to support their friends and neighbors. Remind them that America is a divided country: "Some people don't like or are afraid of Muslims, but most Americans support them." Reassure your children that the ban does not apply to them if they're Americans. But it may apply to friends or relatives in the countries that Trump feels are dangerous.

Mehdi Hasan explains in his essay that Muslim parents under the Trump presidency will need to have "The 'Islamophobia conversation,'" the discussion in which you have to ask your child to be restrained, to be careful when they talk about their faith and their beliefs in public, because, unknown to them, some people see them as a threat.

If you feel that your child may face physical harm from other children or adults in your community, you need to take preventive action by speaking with school administrators or the police officer who is responsible for community liaison.

- Tell your children to walk in a group, not to stray into other neighborhoods, and to seek out adults who might be helpful if threatened (a storekeeper, a police officer, a woman on the street).
- Join with members of your mosque to set up safety patrols for children going to and from school if your community is hostile to them.

- Seek out resources like the Council on American–Islamic Relations for social and legal support.
- Explain to your children and teenagers that a small percentage of Americans are going to be hostile toward them just because they are Muslim, but the majority of Americans will be working to support them in any way they can.
- Let your children know about examples of communities rising up to help their Muslim neighbors, including Jewish congregations offering their synagogues as a place to worship for Muslim communities when their mosques have been burned down, or entire towns rallying to help Muslims rebuild a mosque that has been destroyed.

Special Challenges for Immigrant Families

We are going through a difficult time in our democracy—where people who are frightened about their jobs and their lives are blaming their problems on immigrants. President Trump is supporting and intensifying these people's fears, instead of reassuring them. He has made his anti-immigrant position a major part of his presidency, even though these ideas go against our constitution and repudiate our democracy. Immigrants present little or no threat to the American people. But Immigration and Customs Enforcement (ICE) officers under Trump's new directives have stepped up the enforcement of immigration laws, and have begun rounding up undocumented immigrants without regard for the safety and security of their children. Recently, a thirteen-year-old girl, whose father had come to pick her up at school, recorded her father being arrested by these officers—a traumatizing experience for any child.

Previous restraints on ICE actions—restraints that prevented undocumented immigrants from being arrested at schools, hospitals, institutions of worship, religious ceremonies, funerals, and weddings—are not being recognized. Even in sanctuary cities, where mayors and governors have directly opposed the new immigration procedures and refused to cooperate, ICE officers are arresting immigrants, disrupting families, and subjecting children to emotionally damaging and fearful situations. The Trump administration has boasted about the stepping up of "raids." These kinds of arrests in which immigrants are "swept up" can happen at any time and can even affect immigrants with green cards and visas. Additionally, while President Trump has previously stated he would protect the "dreamers"—young people who came to this country as children, grew up here, and were made a low priority for enforcement under the Obama administration—it is not clear that Trump will keep his promise.

If you are an *undocumented* immigrant of any ethnic background, be sure to make an emergency family plan. Tell your children that you are getting help and seek out legal counsel from the thousands of lawyers who are volunteering their services. Undocumented immigrants from all countries are in grave danger in the Trump presidency. Make sure your children know what to expect. List the people who love and could support them, especially if there is a real possibility that you will need to be separated from them. Consider establishing a power of attorney for your designated caregivers, authorizing these adults to care for your children until they are eighteen.

- Tell your family something like, "I'm going to do everything I can to stay with you and keep our family together, but if I can't, I will try to go into hiding. If they deport me, you will live with mom at your aunt and uncle's house until I can find a way to return to the United States. This would be very sad for all of us, but President Trump is not going to be president forever."

Don't forget that ICE cannot enter your house without a signed warrant, so do not open your doors unless this warrant is passed under your door. Don't speak or sign anything without an attorney present. Kids in Need of Defense (KIND) is a national organization providing immigrant children in the United States with pro bono legal services. The National Immigration Law Center is also devoted to advancing the rights of low-income immigrants and their families.

Special Challenges for Families of Color

Many of us were so thrilled with Obama's presidency—the culmination of fifty years of fighting for civil rights and voting rights and women's rights and gay rights—that we were unprepared for the sharp and extensive backlash among a certain portion of white citizens, who felt their rights were being obliterated and their cultural heritage was being diminished. As a result, we have seen a steady increase in racism, leading up to and precipitating the Trump presidency.

We have forgotten that the abuses of slavery and the unresolved conflicts of the Civil War between the North and the South, between urban and rural areas, between Federalism and states' rights, have left a bitter resentment that has never been fully addressed or ameliorated in our country. Remember that it is not so long ago that black men were being lynched in the South, or Japanese families were being herded into camps, or Jews fleeing the Holocaust were denied entry into our country. The eight years that Obama was president were exceptional, and young children born in this era have no idea what life was like before our first African-American president. Nor can they fully appreciate the radical changes of the Trump presidency and his deliberate attempts to dismantle our federal institutions.

In Kera Bolonik's essay, Linda Villarosa talks about the fact that her son, now seventeen, was nine when President Obama was elected, and describes how he "came of age at a time of political idealism and social change, so his world was shattered" when Trump was elected. Many political analysts see the election of Trump as a symptom, not a cause, of our country's shift to the far-right for several decades. Robin D.G. Kelley, in his essay, reminds us that we do our children a disservice if we do not tell them "the truth about the anti-democratic origins of our political system." He goes on to point out that, "We have at least four decades of globalization; neoliberal attacks on the welfare state, public institutions, and the poor; covert wars; and political and cultural backlash against movements for racial and gender justice." Nevertheless, we know numerous national reports from agencies tracking discrimination have found that, under Trump's presidency, hate speech and hate crimes have radically increased against Muslims, against Latinos, against Jews, and against African Americans.

While parents of color have lived in the shadow of racism all their lives, and are well aware of the ugly side of our democracy, racism has been further licensed during Donald Trump's campaign and presidency to date. Trump's speeches betray a lack of knowledge of the range of African-American experiences in this country, characterizing all African Americans as living in impoverished, violence-ridden inner-city neighborhoods. As a young real estate developer, Trump worked to keep African Americans out of his buildings, ultimately settling with the Justice Department. Trump's selection of Steve Bannon as an adviser, which former Ku Klux Klan leader David Duke called "excellent," and Trump's appointment of Jefferson Beauregard Sessions (previously passed over for a judgeship because of his racist attitudes) as attorney general speak to a regression in American politics to a time when government *pursued* rather than *defended* black Americans (although some might say the police have unfairly pursued them all along). All of these men come to their positions with histories of white supremacy. Even George W. Bush has spoken out publicly to say "I don't like the racism" in the country perpetuated by the Trump administration.

Kera Bolonik writes, in her essay, about Latham Thomas, an African-American mother with a thirteen-year-old son, who worries, "As he gets older, the same people who say my black son is cute now will be trying to put him in jail because they will find him threatening." What should parents do if their children are the targets of racism? When should parents intervene if they hear other people's children spouting bigoted remarks? Should we let children work it out themselves? When should the parents of a child who has said something bigoted be confronted? Topher Sanders's essay opens these questions. He describes hearing a little white girl in a playground tell his five-year-old son that he couldn't play with them because "only white people" could join in. Sanders is surprised that bigotry begins so early in life and notes, "Systemic racism apparently begins at the playground."

Unfortunately, it is true that exclusion, hurt, and cruelty in general are commonplace and begin in early life. Aggression lies within all of us. Big kids prey on little kids, white kids taunt black kids, and vice versa, and Hispanic or Asian or Muslim kids form exclusionary groups for security and safety.

Here are some thoughts for parents to keep in mind in the face of resurgent racism:

- *No baby is born a bigot*: Kids have to be taught bigotry and racism. Alternatively, that means that they can also be taught tolerance and inclusion.
- Model ways for your children to confront racism constructively. Sanders decides that the next time he observes bigotry, he is going to "call out [the] ignorance," both because he wants to stand up for his son and because he wants to "model

for my children ways for them to confront racism without going all scorched earth."

- If your school-aged child is taunted or called the n-word, encourage him to walk away and seek safety. Confronting hostility alone is not likely to be successful. Remind him that nasty people have all kinds of names for all kinds of groups and that he needs adult help to deal with this kind of hostility.
- Find "teachable moments," both for your own children and for others. An important developmental reason to let the little white girl know that what she is saying is wrong is to mobilize her conscience so that perhaps she'll have a feeling of guilt and act differently next time.

In this current racist climate, African-American parents need to focus on their teenagers, who have the passion to declare their views but may not have the judgment to constrain them before a hostile audience. Make sure your idealistic or angry teen hangs out with a group that will support him and help to keep him protected from the worst elements of our society. Joining and working with political activists in civil rights organizations or the Black Lives Matter movement will help to connect him to a meaningful cause. Prepare your teenager for the possibility that he could be targeted by the police, and instruct him that he must never carry anything that could be perceived as a weapon; he must never confront or escalate an argument with someone who is carrying a gun; he should remain respectful of those in power; and the first phone call he is permitted to make should be to you so that you can arrange for legal protection for him. *So, no weapons, no back talk, no confrontation, no disrespect.* Unfortunately, even with these rules, black and brown teenagers remain at risk.

Special Challenges for Jewish Families

American Jews in the last fifty years have become deeply assimilated into our society. While the rise of the alt-right movement has posed an immediate threat to people of color and immigrants, it has also reactivated anti-Semitism. There is no doubt that incidents of anti-Semitism have surged in the United States as a direct result of the Trump presidency.

In his essay, Benjamin Wofford quotes nineteen-year-old Zach Reizes: "What Trump has brought to the surface is, in many ways, the first blatant anti-Semitic experience for the vast majority of American millennials." When Jared Kushner, Trump's Jewish son-in-law, published an op-ed piece in his paper, the *New York Observer*, defending Trump and invoking the plight of Kushner's own ancestors in the Holocaust, Wofford reports that Kushner's extended family fired back, "Please don't invoke our grandparents in vain. . . . It is self-serving and disgusting." And a twenty-three-year-old Jewish writer and member of his staff, Dana Schwartz, wrote to him, "When you stand silent and smiling in the background, [Trump's] Jewish son-in-law, you're giving his most hateful supporters tacit approval."

These young Jews are facing anti-Semitism in a new and powerful way. They are also caught up in a moral and political dilemma because of Israel and their support or lack of support for the Jewish state. President Trump says he is pro-Israel, but what does that mean in the context of the Israeli–Palestinian conflict? Is supporting settlements in Israel a right-wing cause? Haven't secular American Jews always identified with left-wing causes? In addition, young white Jews question whether their pain is legitimate in the context of black men being shot by police all over the country, or Hispanic immigrants being rounded up and seized and deported, or Muslims being refused entry into our country.

During the Women's March, many signs showed common cause

with these groups: "This Wandering Jew Stands with Immigrants," or "This Jew Welcomes Muslims to Our Country," or "This Sign Is Held by a Jew Who Believes That Black Lives Matter," testifying to the fact that Jews identify with other minorities, and have allied with them against bigotry.

If your family is Jewish, or even partly Jewish, you may need to talk about anti-Semitism with your child for the first time. Children and teenagers have recently been exposed to the images of the desecration of Jewish cemeteries and the painting of swastikas on synagogues and playgrounds. You will need to explain:

- For your younger child: "A swastika is a symbol used by people who don't like Jewish people. It's never OK. We are trying to catch the mean guys who did this. We will be all right."

- For your older child: "The Jews have lived for thousands of years in many parts of the world, and often they have been disliked or even hated by other people because they seemed different. While these feelings will always exist in a few prejudiced people, most Jewish people have felt comfortable and accepted in America. But now, with Trump's presidency, all kinds of hatred and violence directed toward different ethnic groups is rising, including toward Jewish people."

- For your teenager: Try to explore the history of antagonism toward Jewish people over the centuries, culminating in the Holocaust. Make sure she understands that there are many varieties of Jewish experience, with some like Hasidim, dressing and living as if they were still in a European ghetto, while other Jews are completely assimilated into American life. It's also important for her to recognize that many people who were not Jewish tried to hide and protect Jews during World War II, and some even gave their lives to save Jewish families.

Explaining Trump to Your Kids

The Power of the People Is Greater Than the People in Power.

—*Sign, Women's March, January 21, 2017*

SOME PARENTS TRY TO PROTECT THEIR CHILDREN FROM TRUMP'S hateful rhetoric by avoiding talking about Trump altogether, or glossing over the news, and turning off the media. But this kind of avoidance is difficult in modern times. Even in restricted communities, like the Amish or the Hasidim, the world seeps in. Media and social media play an all-encompassing role in our lives.

In addition, little children have big ears when it comes to overhearing adult conversations, particularly those that sound worried or fearful. We are all consumed on a daily basis with what we have come to call "Trump talk." Your children hear it, too. If you don't talk to your child about what's going on, she is forced to rely on her own limited understanding and the often inaccurate information she receives from her peers; she will make up what she doesn't know. Remember, when children imagine, they tend to "imagine the worst."

We talk to our kids all the time ("How was your day at school?" "What do you want for dinner?" "Do you want to visit Grandma on Sunday?"). Talking to kids about tough topics requires some extra thought. President Trump is a tough topic, and explaining Trump to your kids means coming up with explanations about both his policies and his personality. When we explain upsetting events to kids (the death of a friend's father, a fire in a house down the street, a terrorist attack) we don't tell them "the truth, the whole truth, and nothing but the truth." Rather, we decide how much information to reveal and what to conceal. When you make this decision, you take into account your child's age, his personality, and his level of understanding. This is true about the Trump presidency, as well. We have to gauge what our children can comprehend and absorb. It's also important to keep the conversation going both ways. Sometimes we conduct monologues with our kids, without giving them a chance to express their views. Make sure to frame a dialogue.

The Four C's and How They Will Help You Construct Your Conversations

In my book *What Should I Tell the Kids? A Parent's Guide to Real Problems in the Real World*, I suggest that an easy way to conduct a conversation with your children about any tough topic is to keep in mind what I call the Four C's—compassion, communication, comprehension, and competence. These four words will help you to explain any disturbing event to your kids, even something as disturbing as President Trump.

- *Show compassion*: "I know you were sad when Hillary Clinton lost the election; I was too, and so were millions and millions of Americans. We are all sad. We've already seen President

Trump make some really bad decisions, but he has a few reasonable people in his cabinet, and maybe they will help him make better decisions."

- *Initiate communication whenever you have a chance*: "What do you think about President Trump building the wall along our border with Mexico?" "Has anyone in school been mean to Miguel or told him he's going to have to leave our country?" "Do the kids talk about Trump?"

- *Increase your child's comprehension of the events he hears and overhears*: "You know, there are a lot of people trying to change President Trump's policies. We're fighting him in Congress and in the courts and on the streets. Millions of people all over the world are marching against his ideas. We're persisting and resisting." Or, "President Trump's election was awful news. He was a terrible choice, and most people didn't vote for him and don't like him, but he won anyway because of our electoral college system, which gives rural areas that only have a small population the same power as urban areas where we have a large population. It's an outdated system, but we're still bound by it."

- *Confirm your child's competence to deal with these events*: "We can do things to help, too. We can march in our town and write to our congressman and meet with other people who don't like Trump's ideas. And by the time you are twelve years old, I hope we will be able to elect a better president."

How can we raise children who are kind, thoughtful, self-controlled, empathic, honest, and responsible when the man who is president displays (on a daily basis) mean, thoughtless, impulsive, self-centered, dishonest, and irresponsible behavior? Trump is every parent's characterological nightmare. Think about it! Would any parent, Republican or Democrat, conservative or liberal, want to raise a child with Trump's personality? Would any school accept him?

But don't be disheartened. Remember, as a parent, you have considerable power on your side. In fact, the continuous attachment between parents and children is forever. This is one of the unique characteristics of human life; no other animal on earth has such a prolonged and meaningful dependence on its parents. This gives us a powerful role in our children's lives. You remain the first line of defense against all outside influences, including the media performances of President Trump.

You probably already limit your child's exposure to television and movies and the computer and phone. Give President Trump and his spokespeople limited air time in your house; remember that Trump is a master manipulator of the media and keeps everyone on edge, waiting for his next disruptive declaration. He deliberately distracts and distorts information. Both you and your children need a break from the media onslaught at times.

Teens can no longer be easily reassured about the world, and the unexpected election of President Trump has shown them that adults around them can be powerless and events can spin out of control. With your young child we relied upon *reassurance*; with your school-aged child, we sought ways to *support and protect* him; but with your teenager, it's important to *increase her knowledge*—of history, of politics, of economics, of psychology. Knowledge is power, and as you expand her mind, her sense of helplessness or hopelessness about the Trump presidency will diminish. Teenagers are able to bring their intellectual maturity and life experiences to bear upon this unfortunate presidency, so this is the time to raise and educate your child citizen. John Dewey reminds us that, "In every generation, democracy must be born anew, with education as its midwife." Most importantly, any child over fourteen years old now will be able to vote in the next election. Don't forget to remind her!

Some Developmental Differences to Keep in Mind

Very young children (birth to three years old) are still relatively cushioned by their parents' care and control, so if they are upset, it is because they are responding to your sadness and anger rather than to the world events that surround you. At this stage, you are the emotional center of your child's world. It is impossible not to be sad and mad, but try not to be despairing or enraged in front of your children. These feelings place too heavy an emotional burden on them. No matter how frightened and disturbed we are by Trump's presidency, we cannot allow our children's lives to be compromised by the current political atmosphere. We have to convey hope for the future to our children; that's a parent's job.

Three- to ten-year-old children are already moving outside of the family circle. They are trying to create a thinking and feeling self, and they are preoccupied with justice and rules as their conscience consolidates. (How many times does your eight-year-old shout, "That's not fair!" or "He cheated!"?) Now your child is exposed to experiences that you cannot mediate—on the street, in school, and with friends. President Trump's ideas (as the parents in this book have revealed in their moving accounts) create new and profound fears for our children, particularly in this age group where they are old enough to recognize danger but still too young to protect themselves.

In Mira Jacob's essay, when her four-year-old son first asks her why she is brown, he is simply observing a difference between his Indian mother and his white, Jewish father, in his multiracial, multiethnic family. Questions about observable differences between himself and others are some of your child's first intellectual inquiries, and Jacob's son is unselfconscious about his interest.

But by the time her son is eight, Trump has become our president. Now fears about President Trump shape his questions: "Does Donald Trump hate all brown people?" "What about brown boys like me?

Does he not like brown boys like me?" President Trump's racist comments have eroded Jacob's son's sense of self-worth. When this happens with your child, you have a chance to place the fault for his self-doubt where it belongs—with President Trump and his rhetoric.

- Be sure to explain that the problem lies with Trump and not with your child: "You know, some men and women and even children can only like people who look like them and think like them. They're frightened by anyone who is different. I'm afraid President Trump is like that; he doesn't like immigrants, he doesn't like people of color, he doesn't like disabled people, he doesn't even seem to like women!"

Children this age are incredibly curious and are likely to ask all kinds of questions. Try to reply as honestly and directly as you can:

- *"Why did people vote for Trump?"* "Sometimes people just want to elect someone new; they wanted a change. Some people felt angry because they lost their jobs and Trump promised to give their jobs back to them."
- *"Why doesn't Trump want to let other people live here?"* "President Trump thinks immigrants are going to cause trouble, and some people agree with him, but we don't. We were all immigrants at one time. Your grandma and grandpa came from Poland; welcoming immigrants is what makes our country special."
- *"Why does President Trump want to build a wall?"* "He's afraid that too many Mexican immigrants want to live here, and he thinks they're bringing in drugs. But most Mexicans are just looking for a better life."
- *"Is Trump going to start a war?"* "There are a lot of people who

work at the White House who don't want a war; it's not just up to him."

Adolescents are natural dreamers, and because changes in their brains now favor abstract reasoning, they are able to bring great commitment to a cause. Respect your teen's determination, her idealism, her curiosity, her social interests, her energy, and her devotion to her friends. These are some of the best aspects of adolescent development. Teenagers also tend to be emotional, with high highs and low lows, pushed by their normal hormonal changes. This allows them to be passionate and to feel things deeply, so events can easily disrupt their emotional balance. Try to help them keep steady, but don't criticize their intensity. Avoid comments such as "You're making such a big deal about this" and "Don't be so emotional; chill out." Your teen's intensity feeds her hopes and dreams.

Puberty and adolescence set in motion the long process of separating from you socially, emotionally, and intellectually. Your adolescent is also beginning to consolidate her identity. In order to do this, sometimes your teen will attack your identity—challenging what you say, what you believe, and who you are. This is natural. Carlos Sandoval talks in his essay about his great-niece, Lexi, who disavowed her mother's Christian conservative values and instead embraces the progressive values of Bernie Sanders. This is a brave move to make as an adolescent; it underscores the developmental push toward separation.

President Trump, in contrast, displays some of the worst aspects of adolescent behavior: he's self-centered, defiant, and doesn't think about the consequences of his actions. He's reckless, impulsive, and stubborn, with poor judgment. He hangs out with a bad crowd (his cabinet and strategists and counselors), he rails against the establishment, he loses his temper, and he doesn't like learning.

Because you don't want your teen to grow up to be narrow-minded, you also need to teach her how to discuss, defend, and debate her political positions. (It can't be us vs. them all the time!) Understanding or empathizing with someone else's point of view does not mean you accept it. It's important to remember that there are plenty of men and women who are not bigots or misogynists but who voted for Donald Trump because they believed he would improve the economy. Other voters believed he would advance a Republican conservative agenda that they support. But some of Trump's supporters from the far-right supremacist side are (as Hillary Clinton stated) "deplorable." Make sure your teenager also knows how to protect herself and walk away from heated discussions about Trump that could turn nasty in our increasingly polarized world.

- Respect your teen's point of view: Listen, don't criticize.
- Engage your teens in exploring complicated political issues and encourage them to stand up for their views, in a safe and appropriate setting.
- Encourage joining like-minded others.
- Discourage provocation.
- Educate your teen to be a good citizen. Make sure her school is teaching civics and that she knows the constitution and the structures of a democracy. Her vote in the next election can change the world.

Using Stories to Communicate: The Reparative Narrative

Stories are the way all cultures teach their kids about the world and about the dangers of the world. ("Little Red Riding Hood," for example, teaches kids to be suspicious of strangers; the story of Aladdin teaches kids to be wary of adults who could trick them.) I call stories that help children to master upsetting events "reparative narratives." A "reparative narrative" about President Trump might be: "In the beginning, no one thought Trump would become president, because he doesn't have any skills or training or experience that qualify him for president. He was just a TV celebrity. But because of that, a lot of people saw him as a powerful businessman, and they hoped he would get them jobs. He is taking destructive actions that go against our constitution, but many of us are trying to stop him. No matter what, we hope he won't be president for more than four years." This narrative is both truthful and useful for your child.

You can help your children gain perspective on Trump's presidency by telling them stories about hard political times in your own life, your parents' lives, or your grandparents' lives:

- "When Tante Nettie lived in Germany, the Nazis came to power and they wanted to take away all the Jews, but her neighbors hid her family in the cellar of their barn and they survived the war."
- "When Tia Rosita was little, her family left Cuba in a boat at night, and she was scared because she couldn't swim and she was afraid the boat would collapse and she would be eaten by sharks, but they made it safely to Miami."

Viet Thanh Nguyen, in his essay, emphasizes we are all storytellers of our own lives, of our American identities, and writes: "I want my son to rise to the challenge of fighting to determine which stories will define our America." He emphasizes the power of language in our lives and explains, "The struggle over the direction of our country is also a fight over whose words will win and whose images will ignite the collective imagination."

Don't underestimate Trump. His repetitive rhetoric has proven to be extremely powerful, and he has mastered the old aphorism, "You inform with reason; you persuade with emotion." Children (ages five to twelve) are emotional creatures. They have not yet developed the capacity for abstract reasoning, nor are they aware of the ways in which they can be manipulated. (This is why we teach them not to talk to strangers, even if they are offered candy, or to go anywhere with a stranger, even if the stranger says he is looking for his lost puppy.) President Trump is a master manipulator. Be sure to protect your children from his influence in the ways we've discussed. He is trying to convince the American people that all of our institutions are corrupt—the courts, the intelligence agencies, the press. This point of view is meant to discourage Americans from participating in their democracy (remember, "We the people") and to establish an alternative reality (his Twitter account) where we are forced to depend on and get our information from Trump (remember, "I, alone"). Attacking the press, scapegoating ethnic groups, fear-mongering, and holding large emotional rallies are the first acts of dictators. Responsible American parents must "resist and persist."

The Call to Action: Facing the Future

If He Builds a Wall, I Will Teach My Children to Tear It Down.
—Sign, Women's March, January 21, 2017

A PLAQUE ON PRESIDENT OBAMA'S DESK IN THE WHITE HOUSE READ, "Hard work is hard." It will be hard work fighting in the streets and the courts and the newspapers and online against President Trump. He is powerful and vindictive, and the people around him appear to have no moral restraints.

In the Trump era, nothing can be taken for granted in our civil discourse—not decency, not respect, not thoughtfulness, not open-mindedness, not honesty, and not civic responsibility. We know that Donald Trump's personality/character produces chaos, but from day to day it is hard to determine which policies the president himself believes in, and which he presents as deliberate provocations—steps in some transactional exchange he is manipulating toward some end that only he knows.

All over our country, millions of people are organizing and

protesting. We are in the midst of an abiding national resistance. As President Trump makes active attempts to dismantle our democracy, the majority of Americans who did not vote for him, and do not agree with him, are fighting back. Civil disobedience has a long and effective history in our country, and you and your children can be part of this historical movement, if you choose.

Preteens and teenagers are developmentally ready to protest. They are interested in ideas, and they have the passion and determination to pursue them. (That's why teenagers raise money for polar bears, convert to Buddhism, become vegetarians, or join the Marines.) They yearn to be a part of something larger than themselves. Talking is necessary but not a sufficient response to the Trump presidency. In order to teach your children "to understand and commit to social and economic justice from an early age," as John Culhane encourages his twelve-year-old twins in his essay, make opportunities for them to join you in your resistance, now.

But as parents, you need to think about how you will incorporate your protest activities into your life. After all, fighting Trump is not a one-shot deal; we will all need to make room in our lives for ongoing, continuous resistance. You and your child/teen need to discuss all the possibilities and, should you decide to engage, set aside time to make phone calls, write letters, show up at congressmen's offices, or join a march.

But don't forget to make room for your kids' ordinary lives. Sometimes parents become so involved in a cause, they forget their kids need their own time to continue their lives. (I've treated sons and daughters of activists whose memories are dominated by being dragged to endless marches and watching their parents be beaten by police.) Our kids are young and unprepared for the ups and downs of political life. As Adam Gopnik points out in his essay, "The lesson of history—one of them, anyway—is that there is no one-way arrow in it, that tragedy lurks around every corner, that the iceberg is there even as the mighty Titanic sails out, unsinkable." He goes on to emphasize that, "Having a tragic view of life is compatible with having a positive view of our worldly duties." So, even if, like many parents in this book, you are understandably disheartened by the Trump presidency, there is still work to be done.

Becoming socially active now, in this historical moment, is a good idea for three important psychological reasons. First, kids do what we do, not what we say, so your kids will identify with you and internalize your values when you provide them with a model of social activism. (The millions of grandmothers and grandfathers and mothers and fathers who protest and march against Trump's policies inspire kids all over the country.) Second, if your children are marching with you, they participate in a common cause, which is in itself thrilling but which also increases the bonds and camaraderie they have with like-minded others. And third, action is an important psychological defense against depression. Most of us have actually been quite depressed by Trump's presidency. Our mood is melancholy; we appear irritable and fatigued, and we feel hopeless and helpless. By engaging in social activism, we convert our passive experience of suffering into an active experience of protest against the unprecedented and frightening political situation we face.

A Final Point

As with anything else in your life as a parent, keep the balance of your child's life (and your own) in mind as you encourage social activism—too little commitment to action in our society has brought us President Trump, but too much commitment can backfire, too, and cause your teenager to exhaust her dedication to justice and her love of liberty. There is life beyond politics; be sure to make room for it.

Acknowledgments

I am so very pleased to have been asked by Diane Wachtell, executive director of The New Press, to provide commentary to these thoughtful and moving essays. All the authors helped me to shape my ideas, and Diane helped me to sharpen my responses.

Thanks go also to Sarah Swong, who participated in creating the structure of the book, and to Rose Worden, my indefatigable assistant, who typed and retyped my endless corrections and additions.

Finally, I want to acknowledge the hundreds of children, adolescents, and parents who worked with me over the years to find ways to deal with troubling issues in troubling times.

Permissions

Ava Siegler, PhD, is a clinical psychologist and the former director of the Institute for Child, Adolescent & Family Studies in New York City, where she maintains a private practice. Dr. Siegler has written a monthly column for *Child* magazine called "Ask Dr. Ava," and she is the author of two award-winning books for parents, *What Should I Tell the Kids? A Parent's Guide to Real Problems in the Real World* and *The Essential Guide to the New Adolescence: How to Raise an Emotionally Healthy Teenager.* She served as a clinical professor of psychology for fifteen years at New York University and Dean of Training at the Postgraduate Center for Mental Health, and has been a forensic consultant to the New York State Supreme Court on issues involving children, adolescents, and their families.

Sarah Swong is a writer and editor based in New York.

Diane Wachtell is the executive director of The New Press.

Celebrating 25 Years of Independent Publishing

Thank you for reading this book published by The New Press. The New Press is a nonprofit, public interest publisher celebrating its twenty-fifth anniversary in 2017. New Press books and authors play a crucial role in sparking conversations about the key political and social issues of our day.

We hope you enjoyed this book and that you will stay in touch with The New Press. Here are a few ways to stay up to date with our books, events, and the issues we cover:

- Sign up at www.thenewpress.com/subscribe to receive updates on New Press authors and issues and to be notified about local events
- Like us on Facebook: www.facebook.com/newpressbooks
- Follow us on Twitter: www.twitter.com/thenewpress

Please consider buying New Press books for yourself; for friends and family; and to donate to schools, libraries, community centers, prison libraries, and other organizations involved with the issues our authors write about.

The New Press is a 501(c)(3) nonprofit organization. You can also support our work with a tax-deductible gift by visiting www.thenewpress.com/donate.